When Forward Feels Backwards

When Forward Feels Backwards

Discovering God's Upside-Down Kingdom and What It Means for Your Work

Jeff Mayhew

RESOURCE *Publications* · Eugene, Oregon

WHEN FORWARD FEELS BACKWARDS
Discovering God's Upside-Down Kingdom and What It Means for Your Work

Copyright © 2025 Jeff Mayhew. All rights reserved. Except for brief quotations in critical publications or reviews, no part of this book may be reproduced in any manner without prior written permission from the publisher. Write: Permissions, Wipf and Stock Publishers, 199 W. 8th Ave., Suite 3, Eugene, OR 97401.

Resource Publications
An Imprint of Wipf and Stock Publishers
199 W. 8th Ave., Suite 3
Eugene, OR 97401

www.wipfandstock.com

PAPERBACK ISBN: 979-8-3852-3768-5
HARDCOVER ISBN: 979-8-3852-3769-2
EBOOK ISBN: 979-8-3852-3770-8
VERSION NUMBER 03/03/25

Cover artwork: *The Upside Down Kingdom* by Hampton Watts ©, used under license from the artist. All rights reserved. Please visit https://www.hamptonwatts.com/ or @hamptonwatts on Instagram to learn more about Hampton and his work.

Scripture quotations marked (ESV) are from the ESV® Bible (The Holy Bible, English Standard Version®), © 2001 by Crossway, a publishing ministry of Good News Publishers. Used by permission. All rights reserved. The ESV text may not be quoted in any publication made available to the public by a Creative Commons license. The ESV may not be translated in whole or in part into any other language.

Scripture quotations marked (NIV) are taken from the Holy Bible, New International Version®, NIV®. Copyright © 1973, 1978, 1984, 2011 by Biblica, Inc.™ Used by permission of Zondervan. All rights reserved worldwide. www.zondervan.com The "NIV" and "New International Version" are trademarks registered in the United States Patent and Trademark Office by Biblica, Inc.™

Scripture quotations marked (MSG) are taken from The Message, copyright © 1993, 2002, 2018 by Eugene H. Peterson. Used by permission of NavPress. All rights reserved. Represented by Tyndale House Publishers.

Scripture quotations marked (TPT) are from The Passion Translation®. Copyright © 2017, 2018, 2020 by Passion & Fire Ministries, Inc. Used by permission. All rights reserved. ThePassionTranslation.com.

Scripture quotation marked (NKJV) are taken from the New King James Version®. Copyright © 1982 by Thomas Nelson. Used by permission. All rights reserved.

Scripture quotations marked (NASB) are taken from the (NASB®) New American Standard Bible®, Copyright © 1960, 1971, 1977, 1995, 2020 by The Lockman Foundation. Used by permission. All rights reserved. lockman.org

Scripture quotations marked (NLT) are taken from the Holy Bible, New Living Translation, copyright ©1996, 2004, 2015 by Tyndale House Foundation. Used by permission of Tyndale House Publishers, Carol Stream, Illinois 60188. All rights reserved.

To my Heavenly Father, who has led me down so many unexpected paths, without which this book would not exist.

To Megan, for recognizing talent in me that I didn't know I had, encouraging me to use what I had been given, and supporting me along the way. You are the love of my life, forever and always.

Don't fool yourself. Don't think that you can be wise merely by being relevant. Be God's fool—that's the path to true wisdom. What the world calls smart, God calls stupid. It's written in Scripture, He exposes the hype of the hipsters. The Master sees through the smoke screens of the know-it-alls. I don't want to hear any of you bragging about yourself or anyone else. Everything is already yours as a gift—Paul, Apollos, Peter, the world, life, death, the present, the future—all of it is yours, and you are privileged to be in union with Christ, who is in union with God.

—1 Corinthians 3:18–23 (MSG)

Contents

1. Introduction | 1
2. Certainty to Mystery | 15
3. Striving to Contentment | 29
4. Capability to Vulnerability | 44
5. Scarcity to Abundance | 58
6. Self-Focused to Others-Focused | 74
7. Changing the World to Self-Transformation | 89
8. Control to Surrender | 105
9. Conclusion | 123

Bibliography | 131

1

Introduction

LET ME START BY asking some questions to see if they resonate with you.

- Have you struggled to make sense of the pain you've experienced in the workplace, like working for a bad boss, being hurt by others, or failure?
- Do you work hard to keep life just the way you want it and feel frustrated when life doesn't go to plan?
- Are you overwhelmed by the problems of the world?
- Is your work life characterized by monotonous routine and a lack of engagement?
- Do you feel like no matter how much you accomplish, it's never enough?
- Are you constantly comparing your success to what others around you have accomplished?
- Do you always feel short of money or time and unable to give to others?

Or perhaps your experience in the workplace is how David Brooks describes it: "Some people . . . taste success, and find it . . . unsatisfying . . . For still others, something unexpected happens that knocks them crossways . . . They are down in the valley of bewilderment or suffering."[1] My own story fell along similar lines. In brief, I went to university, started my first career job, got promoted, completed a professional designation, realized I wanted more of a challenge, and then changed career tracks. This second career track was just the next step in my five-year plan that ended with moving to Europe to pursue an MBA. Except God kept that door closed on me, and then said no to an attempt to move to New York and another plan to be a founder of a private equity firm. During this season, I began to feel stuck in my career; trying to move forward felt more like I was going against the grain or banging my head against the wall. What had been useful to me up until this point ceased to be productive.

Fortunately, by God's leading, I came to understand that this was how my vocation was supposed to be experienced. Far from making a wrong turn, I had merely come to the end of one portion of my life, and God was inviting me to begin another. What was the portion that was ending? And what was the new chapter I was being called into? I had come to reach the end of the immature period of my career, and the next step was to begin the mature phase of my vocation. I don't believe this transition is something that only applies to my own life, however. In fact, I believe this transition from immaturity to maturity applies to everyone, especially Christians. And the experience of feeling stuck at some point in adulthood is one of the clearest markers that we're being invited to enter a new way of being.

What then is maturity in the workplace? Before we answer that question, we first need to answer the question of what the purpose of work is. Unless we have a correct understanding of what work is for, we will fail to have a useful foundation of knowledge that allows us to understand the difference between immaturity and maturity. Often, our careers are referred to as a vocation, which

---

1. Brooks, *Second Mountain*, xiii–xiv.

INTRODUCTION

is derived from the latin word *vocatio*, meaning calling, invitation, or summons. In this lens, we are thus focused on discovering what our calling is, and this is largely dominated by exploring what we want to do. We are trying to figure out what unique abilities and proclivities drive us and what that means for how we earn a living and spend our time. But what we do is only part of a calling, or more accurately, one of our callings. For every Christian, we actually have two callings: a general calling and a specific calling. The general calling is to become like Christ, to "be holy for I am holy,"[2] where our lives model not just Jesus' outward actions but even more importantly, his inner being. We see our general calling as marked by a secure identity rooted in the positional reality of son or daughter of God, the expression and experience of the fruits of the Spirit, a qualitative way of living that Jesus calls ζωή, or *zoé*, demonstrated by the ability to forgive and be forgiven, blessing those who curse us, and suffering. We also have a specific calling, which is our invitation to be a unique blessing to the world in alignment with who God created us to be. This calling is centered on what we do and reflects our individual talents, abilities, giftings, and preferences given to us by God. When we discover our specific callings, we come alive to devote ourselves to a specific mission to bring about the kingdom of God in the present in partnership with the Lord, in a way that only we can. Living in alignment with our specific calling will also cause us to live a life that better reflects Jesus' way of life. Importantly, our two callings reinforce and empower each other. As we take on more of Christ's character in our general calling, we learn how to live our specific callings more effectively. And as we increasingly understand our specific calling on Earth and work towards it, we increasingly experience life the way Jesus experienced it. With this understanding, we see that work is therefore the primary means by which God shapes us into the image of Christ in fulfillment of our general calling, while also being the part of our lives where we discover our unique mission to partner with God in co-creating his kingdom on Earth today.

2. 1 Pet 1:16 (ESV)

When we have a correct understanding of what work is supposed to be, we can then see what our work lives are not supposed to be. For many, career is some combination of identity, security, meaning, or significance apart from Christ, and we therefore have commensurate expectations for what we get out of our work. We thus step into our workplaces chasing titles, power, promotions, money, praise, fame, influence, and impact, either consciously or unconsciously, only to be disappointed by these pursuits. Feeling stuck in our careers is thus an experiential marker that we are beginning to wrestle with things we have incorrectly come to believe are true for our vocations. At a certain point, the tension between what we expect from our careers and what we experience in them becomes untenable. We arrive at a sense of trying to fit a square peg in a round hole as it relates to our work lives. We come to a "realization that [we aren't] making any headway by constantly butting heads with external conditions over which [we have] no control."[3] We're trying to rationalize the world's way of looking at work with God's design for our callings, and we are finding the two are entirely incompatible. Despair, dissatisfaction, and doubt about work are our acquaintances when we reach this point of our professional lives. Our time at work begins to feel like the words of the prophet Jeremiah: "They will sow wheat but reap thorns; they will wear themselves out but gain nothing."[4] At this point, we have two options: we can double down on what has become familiar to us and continue to work by the ways of the world, or we can accept God's invitation to step into working for his kingdom, even if it means embracing a completely different way of working that is unfamiliar to us.

If we accept God's invitation, we thus start to recognize the difference between the assumptions about career that we've taken from the world and what God's design for our work lives is and begin to understand that God wants to accomplish something different in us and through us in our vocations than what we had originally thought. We now see how God wants to shape us into maturity in Christ through our workplace experiences, a reality

3. Buford, *Halftime*, 149.
4. Jer 12:13 (NIV)

that is in direct contrast to a culture that doesn't widely recognize that life is meant to be experienced in different stages and therefore lacks a framework of human or spiritual maturity to guide people through life with. In fact, our culture broadly promotes a continuation of the first half of life well into the later years of life. As Bob Buford writes, "Some people never get to the second half; a good many don't even know it exists."[5] One only needs to look at the dominant themes of wealth and material accumulation, cravings for recognition through career achievements, social media, and community impact, the pursuit of youthfulness through our bodies and clothing, or resistance to any form of commitment (especially relational) that is perceived to bind an individual's freedom to see the promotion of immature aspirations in our society. And what's most alarming to us as Christians is that we tend to adopt our culture's workplace values often without realizing it. As Paul warns the Christians living in Rome, "Don't become so well-adjusted to your culture that you fit into it without even thinking."[6] And nowhere is this truer than how we make sense of our working lives.

We can now return to the question "what is maturity in the workplace?" To start answering this question, we turn to Scripture for the biblical grounding of an immature and mature approach to understanding spiritual maturity and therefore workplace maturity. We begin with the Gospel of John, where Jesus speaks to Peter and says, "When you were young, you used to dress yourself and walk wherever you wanted, but when you are old, you will stretch out your hands, and another will dress you and carry you where you do not want to go."[7] There is a contrast between young and old here, but Jesus is not speaking about age as what makes Peter young or old but by a quality of life, where a young Peter exerts his own will, while an old Peter is led against his will. Paul writing to the Corinthian church speaks to a first half and second half framework in two instances. First, when he describes the Corinthians as spiritual children, driven by their own desires: "But I, brothers, could not

5. Buford, *Halftime*, 27.
6. Rom 12:2 (MSG)
7. John 21:18 (ESV)

address you as spiritual people, but as people of the flesh, as infants in Christ. I fed you with milk, not solid food, for you were not ready for it."[8] Later in the letter, he writes, "When I was a child, I spoke like a child, I thought like a child, I reasoned like a child. When I became a man, I gave up childish ways."[9] Notice the transitions, from child to adult, and from milk to solid food. Finally, the writer of the book of Hebrews affirms this construct when they write, "For though by this time you ought to be teachers, you need someone to teach you again the basic principles of the oracles of God. You need milk, not solid food, for everyone who lives on milk is unskilled in the word of righteousness, since he is a child. But solid food is for the mature, for those who have their powers of discernment trained by constant practice to distinguish good from evil."[10] Pulling all these passages together, we thus see a common theme of an immature stage of life or discipleship and a mature stage.

We can also look to literature to understand the difference between an immature and mature stage of work. Ronald Rolheiser describes our evolution as Christians in *Sacred Fire*, where he describes the fundamental change from the first half of our lives to the second half of our lives as moving from "the struggle to get our lives together" to the "struggle to give our lives away."[11] David Brooks describes the first half/second half construct in terms of climbing the first mountain and the second mountain of life where "the first mountain is about building up the ego and defining the self, the second mountain is about shedding the ego and losing the self. If the first mountain is about acquisition, the second mountain is about contribution. If the first mountain is elitist—moving up—the second mountain is egalitarian—planting yourself among those who need, and walking arm in arm with them."[12] What began as an individualistic journey to explore and express God's invitation to live the life he designed for each of us becomes a life

---

8. 1 Cor 3:1–3 (ESV)
9. 1 Cor 13:11 (ESV)
10. Heb 5:12–14 (ESV)
11. Rolheiser, *Sacred Fire*, 15.
12. Brooks, *Second Mountain*, xvi.

spent trying to live in service to others, particularly in the workplace. Continuing with the theme of an egocentric first phase of life, we can also see it professionally as an evolution from discovering "What do I want to do?" to "Who am I becoming?"

In this construction, work becomes the primary vehicle by which our character is shaped, for better or worse. We spend more of our time at work than anything else in our adult lives other than sleeping, so it stands to reason that God would use the biggest part of our waking hours to form us into Christ. Our ambition then becomes less about what we do or get out of work and more about the type of people we are at work, how we interact with people around us, and how these things change over time, in accordance with Jesus' invitations. David Brooks characterizes entering a phase of work life where "this kind of work is a way of being."[13] This is not to say that what we do doesn't matter. Discovering our specific calling is an indispensable part of our journey as it relates to work. But the journey doesn't stop there. We want to become the kinds of people that God can rule the world with, now.[14]

We see this invitation to maturity reflected in the journey of the Israelites out of Egypt and into the Promised Land. As the land of Egypt was to the Israelites, so the ways that the world views career are to us in the present day. In Egypt, life for the Israelites consisted of working as slaves, carrying heavy burdens, in service of a leader that had no regard for their lives. Approaching our careers with the world's metrics of success results in the same bondage today; we may be free in one sense, but we are still in bondage to what we can produce and what other people see in us. The opposite of Egypt is therefore the Promised Land, where God promises to provide the Israelites (and therefore us) a land flowing with milk and honey, a place where the fruit of the land is provided out of the abundance of God's goodness to Israel, not based on individual efforts, merit, or talent. But as the journey through the wilderness makes clear, we are continually tempted by the allure of the false gods of Egypt (and present-day careerism) to go back

---

13. Brooks, *Second Mountain*, 64.
14. Comer, *Garden City*, 258.

to what we know and are comfortable with instead of following through with God's invitation to experience life and work the way he intended it to be.

We also see this parallelism in the lives of Jesus' disciples. The disciples all meet Jesus in the first phase of their lives. They are full of themselves and grandiose ambitions to build the kingdom of heaven the way they see it. As the Messiah, Jesus is just a vehicle to get the wealth and security they all expected they would get from overthrowing the Romans and being elevated to high positions in a new kingdom of Israel. And how often do we do the same thing now? Jesus is just a special little ingredient that we sprinkle on our careers and ambitions, thinking that we'll get what we want once he's involved and listening to us. We are like the seed amongst the thorns in the parable of the sower, where the "worries of life and the deceitfulness of riches"[15] have overcome our desire to experience work as Jesus intended it to be. We are laying foundations other than Jesus or building on our foundations with materials that will not survive any testing.[16] The progression to maturity thus requires a death to move to the other side. To become fruitful in work like the disciples were requires death; death by Jesus, and therefore to ourselves, but also the death of the ambitions, hopes, aspirations, dreams, and expectations that were not based on God's ambitions for their or our lives. And in the wake of this death flows the Holy Spirit that empowers the disciples to do far more than they could ever have dreamed or imagined when they first met Jesus.

So we want to move to the next stage in our careers. We want to leave Egypt behind and move to the promised land. We want to let go of pursuing our kingdoms and step into receiving God's kingdom. Exchanging the work of our hands for the work of the Spirit. Responding to the invitation to leave behind professional immaturity and step into maturity. What do we then do?

First, we must acknowledge that everything will change. The hardest part of embracing maturity is realizing that what produced success in the past is no longer useful as we grow into professional

---

15. Matt 13:22 (NIV)
16. 1 Cor 3:10–15 (ESV)

maturity as Christians. Moving forward will feel like going backwards because progress is now counterintuitive to how we experienced success up to this point. "It is one of the paradoxes of success that the things and ways which got you there are seldom those things that keep you there."[17] This acknowledgement must be made up front, or we will fail to follow through with the long road of maturity due to unmet expectations. Our guideposts for progress are no longer relevant as we increasingly adopt God's vision for our working lives. It's not that the first phase didn't matter: it's recognizing that it was merely a stepping stone. "The second mountain is not the opposite of the first mountain. To climb it doesn't mean rejecting the first mountain. It's the journey after it. It's the more generous and satisfying phase of life."[18]

It's important to observe that this transition is difficult because there is an interesting conspiracy between how God created life to be experienced in our early adult lives and the world's dominant way of operating that seeks to perpetuate our position in immaturity. When we start our journey of life, the pursuit of something beyond us is the reward pathway that reinforces our choices as we try and figure out what we want to do. For example, we decide we want to work in a profession, so we enroll in university. We spend roughly four years in university working towards being done and then we get a rush of pleasure once that goal's achieved. We then start pursuing a job, or a graduate program, and get another hit of dopamine when we get the job offer or acceptance letter we were hoping and praying for. We want a companion for life, so we start dating, experience a deep rush of feelings when we meet "the one" and get married. We want to experience the world and come home raving about stories from what we saw in far away countries and the people we met there.

Ronald Rolheiser describes it this way:

> Simply put, puberty is designed by God and nature to drive us out of our homes. And puberty generally does its job, sometimes too well! It hits us with a tumult and

17. Buford, *Halftime*, 105.
18. Brooks, *Second Mountain*, xiv.

violence that overthrows our childhood and sends us out, restless, sexually driven, full of grandiose dreams, but confused and insecure, in search of a new home, one that we build for ourselves. And this is a time of much longing and searching: searching for an identity, searching for acceptance, searching for a circle of friends, searching for intimacy, searching for someone to marry, searching for vocation, searching for a career, searching for the right place to live, searching for financial security, and searching for something to give us substance and meaning—in a word, searching for a home.[19]

Or in the more succinct words of Jamie Winship,

When we are young, God is building into us identity.[20]

Making the transition to maturity therefore requires two rebellions, one against our "ego ideal" and one against the "mainstream culture," while also being "brave enough to let parts of [our] old self die."[21] We spend all this time and effort getting our lives together and building careers that we come to think that the rest of life is simply a continuation of the same experience, just to a greater extent. However, a more accurate interpretation of this transition from the first half to the second half of our careers is that we learn to live how the world works before we let go of that rubric and begin to understand how God works. It's as if our job is to learn self-sufficiency before we let go of it to make space for dependence on God. Or put differently, we are creating lives of value that are then given away to others. As Jamie Winship describes Moses' formation in the world of Egypt before his call to lead the Israelites, "God used Egypt to train Moses. Why not be trained by the most powerful nation in the world in order to raise up a new and greater nation?"[22] We go from learning how to build a worldly kingdom to learning how to build an eternal kingdom.

---

19. Rolheiser, *Sacred Fire*, 16–17.
20. Winship, *Living Fearless*, 140.
21. Brooks, *Second Mountain*, xiii–xiv.
22. Winship, *Living Fearless*, 147.

Introduction

The question then becomes, How do we become mature Christians? How do we all prioritize pursuing our general and specific callings in the workplace as Christians? To start, we need to recognize the beliefs about the workplace and vocation that we've inherited from the world. We need to identify the default assumptions and expectations that we unquestioningly carry into our work lives and pursuit of calling and stand them up against the reality of what God has for us. Realizing that our default assumptions regarding work are backwards sets us on the journey to reorienting our lives around the reality of the kingdom and therefore how we make sense of our time at work. As we see these default assumptions, we can then see how short they fall from God's good design for our working lives and thus let go of the false beliefs that keep us stuck in the dissatisfaction of an immature approach to work. We then fill ourselves with the true reality of existence that God reveals to us as it relates to our work, and these truths propel us with new ambitions and ways of being that enable us to increasingly live out our general and specific callings in the workplace, and we thus become mature Christians.

This is the crux of the transition from immaturity to maturity that we see laid out for us in Scripture. Why so many of us fail to progress to maturity in our careers comes from a lack of emphasis on one or both of our callings. And we fail to adequately pursue our general or specific callings because our incorrect beliefs about work are preventing us from stepping into God's invitations for our vocations. Practically, the immature phase of our careers is primarily focused on discerning our specific callings, with the result that we often neglect to turn our attention to our general calling to become like Jesus and its implications for our work lives. We may even be unconsciously working against our general calling to be like Jesus while working out of our specific vocation. In an individualistic society, this is the bucket that most people feeling stuck will fall into. However, there are many who may have progressed far along in developing the character of Christ but find that they continue to lack a sense of specific mission in their vocation and thus are unfulfilled and lukewarm in their profession. Or perhaps it's some combination of both.

Regardless of where we find ourselves, to begin stepping forward into vocational maturity we must now turn to identifying the false beliefs of the world about work and the eternal truths that we must believe to experience work the way God intended. These eternal truths reflect the reality of God's kingdom as revealed to us in Scripture. We see in scripture that it's a present reality[23] that also exists eternally.[24] It's a way of life focused on the pursuit of righteousness,[25] where those who suffer and are persecuted are blessed,[26-27] where material things pale in comparison to the gifts that God gives,[28] greatness is measured by service to others,[29] and every need we have is satisfied.[30] This kingdom is something that's worth devoting our entire lives to,[31] because even though it may appear hidden in the present, it will come to dominate all of existence.[32] It reflects the origin of the world where man dwelled in union with God amongst all of creation.[33]

We need to get a correct understanding of God's kingdom first, because it reveals all the ways that the workplace is not God's kingdom. It provides us with the right vision for how to make sense of our experience and ambitions at work, while also grounding us in the success metrics of God's kingdom instead of how the world defines achievement. A correct vision of the kingdom also provides us with the right grounding for how to discern our unique calling. We need to carry the vision of God's kingdom into our workplaces so that we can see how completely backward the world's vision of work is compared to God's design. We need our

23. Mark 1:15 (NIV)
24. Dan 2:44 (NIV)
25. Rom 14:17 (NIV)
26. Matt 5:3 (NIV)
27. Matt 5:10 (NIV)
28. Luke 12:32-34 (NIV)
29. Matt 20:26 (NIV)
30. Matt 6:25-34 (NIV)
31. Matt 13:44 (NIV)
32. Matt 13:31-32 (NIV)
33. Gen 3:1-3 (NIV)

entire lives to be rooted in God's kingdom, otherwise we'll leave it behind every time we step into our work and see Jesus' words as innocent idealism in the reality of the workplace. We need to bring our work lives in alignment with the kingdom; otherwise we expose ourselves to the disaster of drifting along and passively accepting the tenets and values of society.[34]

A right view of the kingdom is crucially important, but applying it is where the trouble begins. The difficulty of application comes from the fact that our starting point is always the opposite of what Jesus wants for us. The kingdom of God feels backwards to us because its ways of being are completely opposed to our default position. We think our worldly way of being is normal, so the kingdom of God feels foreign. What's required is for the reality of kingdom to become our foundation to such an extent that we begin to see the world's way of life, especially in regards to work, as in complete contradiction to God's design. We need to realize that God's kingdom is not upside down, but *we* are upside down.

Thus, becoming a mature Christian in the workplace requires reorienting our beliefs around the realities of the kingdom and living accordingly. The kingdom realities of maturity come to replace the default assumptions of the world, or immature beliefs, as they relate to our expectations, ambitions, and motivations for work. Specifically, maturity is marked by the transformation of seven distinct immature beliefs into kingdom realities. These seven transitions are summarized as follows:

Immaturity	Maturity
Certainty	Mystery
Striving	Contentment
Capability	Vulnerability
Scarcity	Abundance
Self-Focused	Others-Focused
Changing the World	Self-Transformation
Control	Surrender

---

34. Merton, *Wisdom of the Desert*, 3.

Now, to be clear, we don't magically wake up one night and arrive as completely mature Christians in the workplace that fully believe in the realities of maturity and live in complete accordance with them. There is no twelve-step process that allows us to perfectly live the vision of work in the kingdom of God on this side of heaven. What this framework does provide is a reorientation of our ambitions, and therefore a change in the destination that we are moving towards in our lives, and subsequently, our experience and expectations of work. In the words of Aleksandr Solzhenitsyn, we realize that "the meaning of earthly existence lies not, as we have grown used to thinking, in prospering, but in the development of the soul."[35] We no longer see the journey towards Christian maturity as disconnected from our experience at work but now see the process of becoming mature as foundational to what we do and who we are at work. In addition, this is not a linear process; it occurs in fits and starts, with many steps forward and resets along the way. "The struggle for self-identity and private fulfillment never completely goes away; we are always somewhat haunted by the restlessness of our youth and our own idiosyncratic needs, but the essential default line shifts."[36]

So we've got the framework to move into the second half of our lives. We want to respond to the invitation to "leave the elementary doctrine of Christ and go on to maturity."[37] We recognize that to become mature Christians, we need to become mature in our vocations. Or put differently, we understand that if we fail to approach our work lives in alignment with the kingdom of God, we will refuse the invitation to become mature Christians during our time on Earth. We can now begin working through each area in more detail to help us change the default line of our lives at work.

---

35. Solzhenitsyn, *Gulag Archipelago*, 310–11.
36. Rolheiser, *Sacred Fire*, 18.
37. Heb 6:1 (ESV)

2

Certainty to Mystery

LET ME ASK YOU a question. How engaging is your life? Like truly, and honestly reflect on this question. If you're anything like me, chances are that on serious reflection, life is actually pretty dull. And life is dull despite the fact that you're working a job that you worked really hard to get and are currently working hard in because it relates to your long-term vision of the good life. Your life is likely full of things outside of work that you're doing to get ahead too. Things like developing your fitness level, reading books, attending conferences, taking courses, spending time with friends and family, being mentored, building a side hustle, investing on the side. You get the idea.

Ultimately, you and I both have a vision of how we want the future to turn out, and everything we do today is aligned on making that happen. For most of us, that has a lot to do with money. We think of the house we want to live in, the property it's on, the area of the world it's in. Or we think of traveling to remote locations all over the world and having rich experiences along the way. Maybe there's an activity that you love, and you want to spend every waking minute that you can doing that one thing. I'm only scratching the surface of imagination here.

But pull the thread a little more. So you've got an idea of what your dream life looks like. Great! Now we all work backwards and figure out what we need to do to accomplish that. Say you want a nice suburban life, lots of space, moderate cost of living. Well maybe a job in trades will do, or perhaps a middle management job at a local company. Now try someone else. This time you want a few houses, and you want to travel all over the world. Hmm, sounds like investment banking or maybe law. Last try. Okay, now you want it all. Houses, jets, cars, being in the news. Well, sounds like you're founding the next unicorn tech company.

What do these examples illustrate? That almost uniformly, we assess our career choice based on what we get out of our jobs. If money is the key thing we're after, then boom, insert high-paying career in your life plan and you're off to the races. Or perhaps fame and critical acclaim is what you want: sounds like a career in the arts is for you. Maybe it's power you're after. Not like power to be evil (obviously!) but power to make a positive change in the world. Politics or NGOs are calling your name.

So the die is cast. We've all figured out what we want in life, and we are all signing up to spend the majority of our waking hours chasing a future that we've imagined will make us happy. And that choice doesn't really stop at career choice either. Now we need to think about which company to work for. Or which division within the company. Or the boss we'll have. Or the projects that we work on. We've barely settled on our career choice, and we're already planning out how the next detail in our work lives will contribute to the big dream we have for ourselves.

Let's fast forward this a little. You're now in middle life with a decade or two of experience. You've had some ups and downs. You worked really hard at the beginning of your career but are looking for balance, so you try and figure out how retain your current level of income while working less. Or perhaps you really enjoyed the type of work that you did but could care less about the industry or companies that you did the work for, so you're trying to find a better application of your skill set.

But let's go back to the question at the beginning of this chapter. How engaging is your life? And by engagement, I don't mean overwhelmed with busyness and stress that causes your adrenaline to flow all day out of a fear-based response for survival. I'm talking about waking up every day with a deep delight and curiosity to experience what's to come. If we're honest with ourselves, we're likely experiencing the former and not the latter. We're relying on busyness and stress to indicate to us whether we're engaged or not in our careers. How do I know that? Well ask yourself how you feel when things slow down. When all the activity dies down, do you feel a dull ache of dissatisfaction? When you're running around getting things done with a day that's filled to overflowing, do you feel like this is when life is at its best? And when it's over, do you start scrambling to find something else to give you that feeling again? Henri Nouwen said it best: "The great paradox of our time is that many of us are busy and bored at the same time."[1]

Okay, so if you've tracked with me up until this point, some of the things I'm writing about must be resonating with you. So that leads us to the question "what does this experience tell me?" I believe that the dull ache we're experiencing deep down, the one we only feel when life slows down, comes from choosing our careers based on an expectation of certainty, when what we really desire is to experience mystery.

What do I mean by an expectation of certainty? Prioritizing certainty means choosing our careers (and therefore how we spend most of our time) based on the things we get out of our careers, like money, power, fame, influence, etc. In other words, we're choosing our careers based on their byproducts, not by how we spend our time at work. And the fact is, this way of living is totally normalized by society. The messages we receive while growing up reinforce this constantly. From a very young age, we're told that our responsibility in growing up is to figure out exactly what we

---

1. Nouwen, *Spiritual Life*, 10.

want in life and go out and pursue it. Additionally, we're typically told that this journey is fairly linear and predictable.

Think of the advice given to someone considering a career in law. You go to school for an undergraduate degree, write the LSAT, go to law school, intern at a some legal-related job, start working as an associate or junior clerk, put in the time and hours as a junior, and eventually end up as a partner, judge, corporate counsel, etc. This pattern is repeated ad nauseum: trade school, apprenticeship, ticketed journeyman, foreman in trades; undergraduate degree, MCAT studying, med school, residency, and then full-time practice as a doctor; analyst, then associate, MBA degree, then VP, and finally MD as a banker. And on and on.

This is all common knowledge, isn't it? This is how the world is supposed to work, right? If you want something, you work for it, put in the time, and wait to get what you want. What's wrong with that? Well to start, we have that dull ache we're experiencing, right? Obviously, that tells us something is amiss if we actually listen to it. But if we're listening to it, what is it telling us? To me, the ache tells us three truths about our careers.

The first of these truths is this: living life knowing what the next step is ruins any opportunity for the delight that comes from surprises. Think back to your childhood. Remember what that was like? How often were you surprised and filled with wonder? Like the time you first rode a bike on your own, your first trip to see a new city, or when you tried a new flavor of ice cream. There's this sense of novelty and excitement that permeates our lives as children, and that has a lot to do with not thinking very much about what's coming up next. Kids are always late to things because they're engrossed with whatever is in front of them. I remember constantly being late to the dinner table because I was busy playing with friends or building something. I imagine many of you have similar memories.

In contrast, as adults, it appears that our standard operating procedure is to remove any sense of novelty or mystery from our lives. We plan excessively and imagine what things will be like before the moment even happens. Especially so in our careers. We dream about potential careers we want to pursue and the type of people we'll be when we achieve them. Or we imagine what our lives will look like once we get promoted a few steps up the ladder and have made it.

However, it seems that reality rarely (if ever) lives up to our idealized vision of it. Think of the last time you achieved a goal where everything went perfectly according to your plan. How did you feel after you achieved it? Other than a temporary "high," did it turn out to be anything other than a letdown? Or how about when you imagined making a change in your career, completed a tremendous amount of networking and personal development to make the change, and then started the role you had been picturing yourself in? I'm pretty sure the real job didn't live up to your expectations either.

Needless to say, it seems evident to me that our excessive focus on planning and anticipating what's coming next in life seems to rob us of the delight of what comes when we encounter things in life that were entirely unexpected. What if instead of perfectly orchestrating our daily, weekly, monthly, and yearly plans, we chose to live one day at a time and let each day constantly surprise us as we slowly move into chapters of our life that we could never have imagined of our own accord?

The second truth that our ache of dissatisfaction tells us is this: engineering our lives to focus on what we get of our careers leaves us disconnected and numb to how we spend the majority of our time. Let's go back to childhood. Not only are kids not thinking of what's coming next in life, they're also losing track of time because they're completely invested in what's in front of them. When a child is playing with friends or their favorite toy, nothing else matters to them. They don't even bother thinking about what comes next because what they have in that moment is at least, if not more than, enough to capture their entire attention span. It should be no surprise to us that Jesus exhorts us to become like children.[2] In fact, Jesus even goes so far as to say that a requirement for entering the kingdom of God is becoming like children. However, the

2. Matt 18:3 (NIV)

invitation to be childlike in a work context is not to reverse course and start behaving like a child but to retain the quality of life that children live—free of worry, fear, anxiety, focused on the present, and giving entirely of self—and apply it to our adult lives.

Isn't it odd then how adulthood is the polar opposite of life as a child? We're constantly planning, scheduling, or coordinating our routines so we can squeeze everything into the limited amount of time that we have. Even weirder is that instead of enjoying all the things we have planned for ourselves, we tend to focus on what the next thing in the calendar is, or what the next thing we have to do is. We are completely inattentive to *whatever* is in front of us to the point that we are hardly paying attention to life as it happens.

If we're at work, we're probably thinking about what we're going to do after work. Or maybe dreaming about the next job we're looking for. And then if we're not at work, we're thinking about all the things we need to do at work once we get back to our computer. It's as if we are forever planning our future in a vain attempt to control it, while life as we know it completely passes us by. Is it any wonder why we feel so empty when life slows down? We've spent the entire busy period of our life cut off from our experience of life as it happened, and it's only when we let our body catch up to our mind do we realize that none of what we did actually meant anything to our soul. David Brooks sums it up well: "Your ego prefers certainty to uncertainty, predictability over surprise, clarity over ambiguity. Your ego always wants to shroud over the barely audible murmurings of the heart."[3]

The final truth that we lose sight of is that our quest for certainty leads us to avoid taking risks or choosing paths in life where the outcomes are unknown. Why is avoiding risk a bad thing? Aren't we supposed to prudently manage or completely avoid risk to prevent ourselves from losing what's most important to us? Think about all the businesses and professions devoted to risk management. We have home insurance, life insurance, credit risk management, investment risk management, business risk management, and health risk management—all devoted to making sure

3. Brooks, *Second Mountain*, 43.

life isn't full of surprises and things go to plan. We even have colloquialisms in our language about risks: "don't put all your eggs in one basket" or "one in the hand is worth two in the bush." In short, we naturally assume that avoiding risk or doing the "smart" thing is the dominant lens with which we're supposed to design our lives.

As a result of this pursuit of certainty our default is to choose the predictable path in life and ignore the reality that "risk is inherent in the Christian faith."[4] We do the wise thing consistently: avoid situations where things might not go our way, choose pursuits without surprises, take the "safe" route where probability and time of arrival is certain rather than "go into the world and to make disciples of all nations which is bound to involve us in risky ventures, whether we travel to some remote part of the world to do mission work or cross the street to befriend a neighbor."[5] In Bob Buford's words, "Everything seems to conspire to keep us where we are."[6] Yet this approach is at odds with our deepest desires. Deep down we crave meaning, significance, impact, and influence. We want to make a difference. We want to see reality bend closer towards our imagination. We want to see what we are truly capable of. But none of these things can occur when our default position is safety and security. In short, "Life seems more comfortable in known, familiar territory, even when we are fairly certain something better awaits us out there."[7]

When we attempt to find the transformative without risk, we encounter the illusion of change and focus our attention on quick fixes. This can include focusing our attention on surface level changes like political parties, leaders, marketing slogans, or social media trends, when the underlying causes are ignored. Another example is trying to get involved in projects, companies, or social movements that have substantial momentum or powerful and influential people involved, as we believe that participating in something where success is assured will satisfy our longings. Or

4. Sittser, *Water from a Deep Well*, 257.
5. Sittser, *Water from a Deep Well*, 257.
6. Buford, *Halftime*, 105.
7. Buford, *Halftime*, 105.

lastly, we avoid doing the right thing in individual moments because of the personal cost that we will pay. As psychologist Edwin Friedman put it, "American civilization . . . has perverted the elan of risk-taking discovery and pioneering that originally led to the foundations of our nation. As a result, its fundamental character has instead been shaped into an illusive and often compulsive search for safety and certainty."[8]

We thus find ourselves locked in a cage of pursuing certainty in our lives but experiencing a lack of delight and surprise, a consistent disconnection and numbness to the present, and an avoidance of risk. We know the status quo is not fulfilling, so where does that leave us? What is the next step?

The next step is embracing mystery. Why mystery? Because certainty is the opposite of what we crave. Predictability, certainty, and perfectly executed plans may be what our mind tells us we should want, but deep down our hearts are telling us that the thrill of adventure filled with risks, failures, and triumphant success is actually what we're longing for. The type of life where the next step is a mystery until you're standing on top of it. The type of life where we are fully engaged with each moment. The type of life that fills to the brim and then overflows whether external circumstances are delightful or dismal. The type of life where we are fully invested in people and pursuits, without any concern for what we might lose in that position.

Mystery is a style of living where we are all in, without any requirements to get what we think we want. Mystery doesn't exist in a vacuum however. Mystery doesn't exist as an impersonal force that merely adds randomness in our lives to keep us guessing. Mystery doesn't bring us a sense of vitality because we lack a sense of the future. Mystery fills our soul not only because of how it brings radiance to our present moments but because it brings adventure and growth. Mystery without these two things would merely lead to endless confusion, detachment from reality, and an existential coldness that would be the opposite of what we're seeking.

---

8. Friedman, *Failure of Nerve*, 59.

But mystery with adventure is where things begin to click for us. Why is that? Because adventure has a destination. The destination of adventure is our calling to become like Christ, become who we were created to be, and accomplish the works that God has set out for us. Adventure has a mission that makes meaning of the low moments, the setbacks, the failures, and the disappointments that come with mystery. Adventure keeps our chins up when our expectations aren't met. Adventure gives us the fortitude to keep moving forward when the going gets tough. Adventure gives us hope that when we feel lost we can know it's only part of the journey, not the entire trip. Adventure gives us grace to make mistakes because after we fall down, there can be something around the corner that will have us jumping for joy again.

As we give ourselves to the mystery of life and allow adventure to move us forward through life, we see ourselves grow into people that we never thought we could become. In ignorance, we think we can grow by designing circumstances so that we can achieve a specific outcome. Or put differently, we conflate our ability to control circumstances as evidence of our growing capacity, when in fact our ability to control anything merely demonstrates the limits of our abilities. It's only when we're faced with aspects of life that we never saw coming and require us to overcome things we didn't think we would be able to that we actually grow beyond our current station. It's only when we embrace mystery that we can see that we desire meaning, significance, impact, and influence, yet consistently settle for situations that only reinforce our smallness rather than expose ourselves to circumstances where we can see what we are truly capable of.

So if you want a life that is all in, where you embrace mystery, experience adventure, and grow yourself, you'll likely be asking yourself how you do it. The idea of everything sounds great, but what does that actually mean in practice? First and foremost to embrace mystery in your life, you have to face your fears. As pastor and author John Ortberg puts it:

> If you want to walk on water, you've got to get out of the boat. I believe there is something—Someone—inside us

who tells us there is more to life than sitting in the boat. You were made for something more than merely avoiding failure. There is something inside you that wants to walk on the water—to leave the comfort of routine existence and abandon yourself to the high adventure of following God. So let me ask you a very important question: What's your boat? Want to know what your boat is? Your fear will tell you. Just ask yourself this: What is that most produces fear in me—especially when I think of leaving it behind and stepping out in faith?"[9]

Fear is what keeps us searching for certainty. We mistakenly aim for the predictable for fear of the unknown, but in doing so avoid mystery, adventure, and therefore growth. As a result, we allow our fear to obscure our deepest desires. As David Brooks writes, "What would you do if you weren't afraid? Fear is a pretty good GPS system; it tells you where your true desires are, even if they are on the far side of social disapproval."[10] Fear also prevents us from recognizing new opportunities or expanding the realm of the possible, or in Jamie Winship's words, "Fear shuts down creativity and the reception of new ideas."[11] So if we want to live the life that our hearts desire, we have to face our fears to allow us to move past the paralyzing feeling that keeps us disengaged and discontent.

But facing our fears is only the start. Facing our fears only gets us out of the boat, as John Ortberg described it. The journey doesn't end when we get out of the boat. In fact, it's only the beginning. Now we need to figure out what our mission is—the destination that makes our journey in life an adventure. Our unique vocation that only we can fulfill. At this point, additional questions can help us understand our destination too. Questions like, What makes me feel alive? What do I enjoy doing even if I'm not successful? How would I like to spend my time if no one was watching? What work would I be satisfied with even if it didn't produce external markers of success? What am I equipped to fix that no one

---

9. Ortberg, *If You Want to Walk on Water*, 17.
10. Brooks, *Second Mountain*, 119.
11. Winship, *Living Fearless*, 32.

else is? Once we answer these questions, all that's left is to "begin as all things do, with one small step," understanding that "only God knows where that step will lead."[12]

And as we begin to figure out our destination and move towards it, we can begin to experience how the mystery of life begins to shape us into something beyond the person who began the journey. We begin to discover the talents and abilities that had lain hidden for years or decades, but upon activation, fill us with a sense of significance that no accomplishment or well-executed plan could ever match. As Bob Buford writes, "Christ meets us and works with us in the confusion, and in the valley of the shadow of death, in the tunnel of chaos when the familiar landmarks have disappeared."[13] We become the person we felt we knew we could become, but at the same time, become someone we never could have imagined of our own accord. We realize that "God is forcing [us] up to a higher level: putting [us] into situations where [we] will have to be very much braver, or more patient, or more loving than [we] ever dreamed of being before. It seems to us all unnecessary: but that is because we have not yet had the slightest notion of the tremendous thing [God] means to make of us."[14] We become different people too. We become fearless people. Fearless people have been set free from the terror of fear to walk side by side with God wherever he leads. As a result, "Finding work to do that makes your fearless will make you unstoppable. Setbacks will become stepping stones to a more refined vision of one's vocation. The wrongs done to you will become opportunities for cultivating wisdom necessary for your next iteration, making you stronger, more resilient, less fragile."[15] But, "We can only become fearless by following God into fearful situations and experiencing his love and protection."[16]

---

12. Sittser, *Water from a Deep Well*, 279.
13. Buford, *Halftime*, 93.
14. Sittser, *Water from a Deep Well*, 137.
15. Beck, "Anti-Fragile Brendan Eich."
16. Winship, *Living Fearless*, 78.

Yes, we truly desire mystery. Mystery brings adventure and growth, but embracing mystery is in direct contrast to our default way of living that lets fear keep us stuck in a life of meaningless and unengaging certainty where we get what we think we want. There is much to ponder, and much work ahead for us to redirect our lives towards what our hearts truly desire. But before embarking, I will end with one of my favorite passages of the Bible, which encapsulates so well the posture we seek and the blessing that comes with it. "Abraham, when called to go to a place he would later receive as his inheritance, obeyed and went, *even though he did not know where he was going.*"[17] It's this attitude of setting out without knowing where we are going that marked the efforts of many Christian missionaries, whose "work progressed slowly and unpredictably and mysteriously [and] made little decisions every day to do the will of God as they knew it; they took little risks-as well as a few big ones that set them on a course leading to adventure, achievement, and influence; they chose to devote their time, talent and energy to God, refusing to put limits on what God would do with them."[18] Regardless of what type of work we do, we are all invited to take small steps every day towards destinations we can't see based on the leading of the Lord. May we all be so blessed as to embark on own adventures, not knowing where we are going.

AUTHOR'S REFLECTION

Ever since I can remember, I have been a planner. Whether it was my day-to-day routine, my weekly schedule, my vacations, or my long-term goals, I always had a plan. And not only did I have a plan, it was meticulously laid out, well-researched, and thought through from beginning to end, leaving nothing to chance. As a result, I got a lot of satisfaction in the present based on whether I felt I was making progress towards my long-term goals. I would also think a

---

17. Heb 11:8 (NIV)
18. Sittser, *Water from a Deep Well*, 278.

lot about the end state that I was aiming for, trying to get a taste of my imagined pot of gold at the end of the proverbial rainbow.

A great example of this was my "five-year plan" that guided the first part of my career. I started as a commercial banker, but then I wanted to complete my CFA designation, transition to private equity, get promoted, go to an international MBA program, and then I'd finally live the life I desired by jet-setting across the world as I invested in the best companies. Another example is that I've always dreamed of starting my own investment firm. In my recent life, working at a hydrogen fuel cell company, I believed that I would get promoted to a director position, then to a vice president, at which point I'd finally have the skills and capabilities to justify setting out on my own. The commonality for both positions was that I assumed that being on my current step of my imagined path of certainty would inevitably lead me to my far-off goal.

Oh, how wrong have I been! Not only did I not get into the MBA programs I had applied to earlier in my career, but I didn't even make it to the director level before getting let go by my former employer. Slowly, I'm learning to believe that this is actually how God wants our lives to be experienced. I have not been able to find one example in the Bible of a person's life being characterized by a predictable path from someone meeting God and fulfilling their calling. In fact, it seems that the most common route is a highly unpredictable journey of tremendous ups and downs, seeming dead ends, and a resolute sense of not understanding where God is leading the person in the grand scheme of things. It seems like we've completely lost that reality in a modern society that has tried to insulate us from so many of the vagaries of life.

As I embrace mystery, I'm beginning to see that the unpredictable and unknown path is actually the one that God is calling me to. If I can see the specific outcome of a choice or create an easy-to-follow plan that will result in me getting what I want, I have started to become skeptical of that being the path that God would lead me into. Rather, if I'm getting a sense that God wants me to do something that is filled with the risk of failure, is completely outside of a proven path of success, or may even make me look foolish in the world's eyes, then I increasingly believe that those are the promptings of the Spirit. It's these promptings where God wants to lead me into something completely new that will completely change my perspective of how he works, while leading me into deeper relationship with him at the same time. And it's these promptings that I'm beginning to understand contain the quality of life that we all deeply desire from the bottom of our souls.

DISCUSSION QUESTIONS

1. Do you agree that embracing mystery is something we should aspire towards in our careers? Why or why not?
2. Where are you at in terms of embracing mystery in your work?
3. Take some time to pray and ask the Lord to reveal how he's calling you to step towards embracing mystery in your work life.

3

Striving to Contentment

DOES IT FEEL LIKE you're always in a rush from place to place, activity to activity, or project to project? Does it ever feel like everything in life is riding on your shoulders, and if you don't deliver, everything will fall apart? Are you constantly chasing "the next big thing," accomplishing your goals, and checking off your to-do list but always feeling the same? When you get whatever it is you have been chasing, is it ever anything other than a momentary experience? And does the "high" of getting what you want go down over time, not up? Perhaps your experience is that you are "always finding out that beyond the pot of gold at the end of the rainbow, there's a sort of emptiness."[1] Or to encapsulate all these experiences in one question, do you find yourself always focused on something that's beyond or outside of you and never present with what's in front of you?

If you answered yes to any of these questions, you're not alone. If anything, you're like most people, so there's a sense of comfort knowing that your experience is not an isolated example. However, that doesn't mean that this way of living is how life is

---

1. Buford, *Halftime*, 86.

supposed to be. John Mark Comer makes the case that "hurry is the root problem underneath so many of the symptoms of toxicity in the world."[2] This toxicity isn't just an aspect of the external world that we live in but a toxicity that's deep inside us. Only this toxicity isn't a sharp pain that's at the top of our senses but more like a low-grade headache that covers most of our lives, whether we know it or not.

One symptom of a life of hurry that is particularly relevant to our career life is hurry sickness, which is defined as "a continuous struggle and unremitting attempt to accomplish or achieve more and more things or participate in more and more events in less and less time."[3] But what does hurry sickness have to do with my career? Aren't we supposed to be busy? Shouldn't I have a calendar full of meetings? Shouldn't my day be filled with completing work to meet deadlines? If I want to move up the ladder, don't I need to show that I can take on a lot and get it all done on time? If I'm a responsible person, shouldn't I be able to get it all done on my own without relying on others? Isn't hurry sickness the inevitable outcome of being an ambitious person that wants to succeed in their career?

Short answer, no. Long answer, also no, but given what we were taught growing up, it's not a surprise that we ended up in this place. So how did we get here? Largely through our journey from adolescence to adulthood. At the beginning of life, we are primarily helpless and rely on the efforts of others to meet our basic and aspirational needs. But, as we progress into young adults, we begin to assume responsibility to meet our own needs. This starts out small, like completing homework or doing chores around the house, but quickly moves beyond simple tasks to more consequential tasks and responsibilities. Things like deciding what to study in school, earning enough to care for our own individual needs, saving up for major purchases, etc. A big part of what is going on during this phase of life is we are developing the skills necessary

---

2. Comer, *Ruthless Elimination of Hurry*, 19.
3. Rosenman and Friedman, *Type A Behavior and Your Heart*, 33.

to become a self-sustaining person but also discovering our own individual capabilities to build a life that we desire.

As noted in the introduction of this book, this phase of our lives is the "struggle to get our lives together,"[4] a struggle that is marked by the process of finding our own identity along with fulfilment and peace. Importantly for us, what marks this phase of life is longing and searching: "Searching for an identity, searching for acceptance, searching for a circle of friends, searching for intimacy, searching for someone to marry, searching for a vocations, searching for a career, searching for the right place to live, searching for financial security, and searching for something to give us substance and meaning—in a word, searching for a home."[5] These are all good and healthy things that we're supposed to pursue and form a key part of maturing into healthy individuals. However, our error comes from not exiting this phase of life. At a certain point, the struggle to get our lives together is supposed to end, and we move on to the next chapter. Except we don't. Our default is not only to stay stuck in this state of searching and longing but to double-down on it and pursue it to an even greater extent than when we started. What once was a journey to find our own home becomes looking for a home when we've already found it, with diminishing returns to boot.

Flip back to the questions at the beginning of this chapter. Why do these experiences resonate with us? Because the majority of us have reached the life we built for ourselves or felt called to, only to continue trying to conjure up more of that feeling of accomplishment that affirmed our choices when we were young. In our journey of becoming adults, we came to believe that achieving our goals and building a life for ourselves was the end result and not simply the means to get us out of adolescence.

So it shouldn't be any surprise that upon achieving all the goals that we set out for ourselves, we simply just put more in front of ourselves and chase after them. Except now the goals are bigger and grander. Where at first we were happy just to get on the

---

4. Rolheiser, *Sacred Fire*, 15.
5. Rolheiser, *Sacred Fire*, 16.

first rung of our career ladder, now we're figuring out how to get to middle management, a senior leadership team, or the c-suite. Where at first we were happy with a condo or a basement suite shared with friends, now we're scheming our way into a townhouse, house, or oceanside villa. And not only do we have much larger goals to achieve (which, as I've already mentioned, don't deliver the same payoff as they used to), now we're investing our happiness and satisfaction in life on them. By continuing to stay in the immature phase of adulthood, we unconsciously adopt the way of believing that what we truly desire is always one step ahead of us. This way of thinking sounds a lot like this:

I will be happy when _____.

For example,

I will be happy when I own a home
I will be happy when I get promoted
I will be happy when I finish school
I will be happy when I run my own business
I will be happy when I travel to a certain country
I will be happy when I retire
I will be happy when I get married
I will be happy when the big project is done

We may not say any of these phrases verbally or even consciously in our minds. But based on how we actually live our lives, we believe this to be true: hook, line, and sinker. It doesn't help that Western civilization seems to reinforce this way of thinking either. So much of our modern economy is based on selling the idea that what we deeply desire is just one step beyond where we currently are, where our "well-being is predicated on an aspirational dynamic fueled by dissatisfaction."[6] We just need one more consumer product, or one more self-help technique, one more piece of technology to improve it all, or if we have got it all, now we fear missing out on something that someone else has. We "seem to be in constant need of activity and success" where "the frenzied

---

6. Adubato, "Metaphysical Promise of the Consumer Society."

pace of [our] lives poses a threat to spiritual health."[7] And this is all communicated constantly by modern marketing! So, we find ourselves longing for a "home" that we're already living in, believing that we can find what we long for by attaining something outside of us, constantly placing new goals, accomplishments, and material items in front of us thinking they're what we're longing for, and hurrying through life trying to accomplish it all because the next thing just never seems to satisfy.

This way of living has a name: striving. Striving is that slightly empty feeling in all of us, that causes us to incessantly search for something outside of us to fill it. Striving is that inability to rest because of the endless list of goals and tasks we need to accomplish to get what we want. Striving causes us to be "blinded by our desire for ceaseless motion, for a constant sense of achievement, famished with crude hunger for results, for visible and tangible success, [where we] work [ourselves] into a state in which [we] cannot believe that [we] are pleasing God unless [we] are busy with a dozen jobs at the same time."[8] Striving is spreading ourselves too thin because we believe we need to do it all to achieve the life of our dreams. Striving is chasing the next big thing or the decisive moment that propels us into the place where we've "made it." Striving is the pressure we feel to have a certain amount of success by a certain age or milestone, based on internal or external expectations. Or as Nathan Harrison describes it, striving is "searching for meaning in something that you won't actually find meaning in."[9]

But striving isn't just the search for our own version of the promised land. Striving is marked by combining that continuous search with positioning ourselves as the protagonist that makes it all happen. We not only have a destination to reach, but it's entirely up to us to arrive there. We believe that without our efforts, none of what we long for will occur, and if we're behind the level of success we think we're supposed to have, we need to double down on our efforts today to catch up to some imaginary race. This ultimately

---

7. Sittser, *Water from a Deep Well*, 94.
8. Merton, *New Seeds of Contemplation*, 206.
9. Harrison, *Sabbath as Resistance*, Oct. 30, 2022

sets us up to live in a hamster wheel, because as we continue to chase after what we believe will lead us to joy, we work harder and harder at an ever-expanding list of wants. Except that instead of satisfying us, our growing list of accomplishments and achievements only leads us to feeling increasingly drained.

That's why striving is so exhausting. Not only do we have to figure out all the things we need to do to build the life that we desire; we have to finish all the work to make it happen, fix all the problems in the way, and then navigate all of the unanticipated challenges that we hadn't thought of in advance. Is it any wonder why burnout and exhaustion are so prevalent in modern society? Not to mention the pervasiveness of anxiety and depression despite a civilization that is the wealthiest in history, one where low-income individuals enjoy daily comforts that royalty two hundred years ago couldn't have dreamed of. Simply put, when we live out of a posture of striving in life, we are assuming way too much responsibility for our own destiny than we were ever meant to shoulder. And the amount of people at their breaking points on a physical and emotional level evidences the pervasiveness of this mentality.

Finding ourselves stuck in a life of striving is an important transition point. We've grown up learning to set goals for ourselves and achieving them through our own actions, yet we find ourselves hitting a wall when we continue to apply that way of living as we mature in age. We believe there's something beyond us that is where we'll find happiness, but our methods for attaining it seem woefully inadequate. So what do we do?

We start by letting go of what we're chasing for ourselves and thereby cease from the activities that are burying us into the ground. To get through this wall, the answer is no longer more but less. And we need to take ourselves out of the driver seat, as scary as that might be. As Pete Scazzero puts it: "Going through the Wall breaks something deep within us—that driving, grasping, fearful self-will that must produce, that must make something happen, that must get it done for [ourselves] (just in case [God] doesn't)."[10]

10. Scazzero, *Emotionally Healthy Spirituality*, 112.

A big part of this transition is marked by letting go of the "driving, grasping, and fearful self-will." But letting go is only half of the solution. We not only need to let go of our way of striving, but we need to grasp firmly on the truth that overcomes striving. That truth is the practice of contentment.

Where a life of striving implicitly says that our happiness is outside of us and it's up to us to capture it, contentment tells us that we already have everything we need inside of us for joy and peace today. We no longer need the promotion, the pay raise, the new car, a new wardrobe, to be recognized for our position, to have people notice us for our success, etc. Whatever we have today is enough, and we no longer need to think about anything else. As the apostle Paul writes, "Godliness with contentment is great gain. For we brought nothing into the world, and we can take nothing out of it. But if we have food and clothing, we will be content with that. Those who want to get rich fall into temptation and a trap and into many foolish and harmful desires that plunge people into ruin and destruction."[11] Now many will recoil at this passage. They'll tell themselves that they don't really want to get rich; they just want something as simple as owning a home, selling their business for a certain amount of money, being able to vacation, or attaining a certain level of seniority in their career. And they'll justify this by saying that whatever they want isn't as high as what other people have, so it's obviously not "rich" in their own judgment.

But pay attention to the end of the passage. The fruits of the way of this way of living plunges people into ruin and destruction. When we hear these words, we tend to associate ruin and destruction with something disastrous like a house burning down, or a natural disaster, or maybe an unwise business decision that causes someone to lose it all. However, what this passage is really talking about is the interior quality of one's life, or put another way, how we experience the present. And as we've talked about in this chapter, a lot of our present experience is a combination of exhaustion, anxiety, and depression—clear experiential markers that our way

---

11. 1 Tim 6:6–9 (NIV)

of living has already plunged us into ruin and destruction, because we're falling short of the way life is meant to be experienced.

So, it's clear—the antidote to our longings is not more of whatever is on our list like we had originally thought, but replacing that list with a new one highlighting everything that we already have. Importantly, for contentment to truly bless us, we can't settle for highlighting external or surface-level blessings to find contentment in either. We need to press deeper into recognizing our relationships, our inherited position in life, personal abilities and competencies, and our interior life to truly recognize how much we possess today.

In recognizing the vast riches we already have, we can also accept the invitation to recognize God as the giver of every good gift in our lives throughout the past, present, and future, while taking ourselves out of the driver's seat in ensuring that we attain the gifts we want to earn for ourselves. A big part of this process involves a deep humbling of our hearts, as we come to accept our own limited perspective as humans in comparison to God's infinite being. With this revised posture, we can then come to see how little our own ambitions for ourselves are, in comparison to what God actually wants to bless us with. As the apostle Paul, this time writing to the Ephesians, says, "Now to him who is able to do immeasurably more than all we ask or imagine, according to his power that is at work within us."[12]

As Paul makes clear, God is able to do far more than we can imagine, and far more than our individual efforts are capable of producing. A life that is more than you can ask or imagine! Who wouldn't want that?! But it's this reality that we refuse to believe in when we settle for a life of striving. The "immeasurably more" of God isn't a supercharging of what we already want, however. It actually means opening ourselves up to let God go beyond what we can actually think of for ourselves through our limited human perspective. But, to catch even a glimpse of what God wants to do for us requires us to first take a step out of the pressure cooker of striving and take stock of all that we've received from God already.

12. Eph 3:20 (NIV)

And as we become content in all that we have, we're able to accept the truth that we are often pretty bad at figuring out what is best for ourselves. Contentment shows us the folly of living for our own selfish ambitions. And it's these selfish ambitions that we try to realize for ourselves in striving that lead us to a subpar experience on a daily basis, and also happen to be poor substitutes for the life that God actually wants to bless us with. In contentment, we create the space to understand what our deepest desires are and then go to God to see them fulfilled. Contentment does not cease from action, but it changes how we channel our desires, replacing ourselves as the fulfillment of our true desires with God as the fulfiller.

Paul re-emphasizes the importance of contentment when he writes, "Dear Titus, legitimate son in the faith: Receive everything God our Father and Jesus our Savior give you!"[13] Notice the emphasis on receiving in Paul's encouragement to Titus. Receiving is the opposite of striving and therefore synonymous with contentment. If we are truly children of God, we have already become co-heirs with Christ of God's entire kingdom. If that is true, we are in fact rulers of all of God's possessions today, not only when we see him face-to-face and regardless of our economic status. So, if we actually believe we are inheritors of the kingdom today, we can thus recognize God's desire to give us a life that is beyond our dreams as a completely free gift, one that is completely unattached from the effort, merit, or right actions that we use to justify outcomes with in striving. For many of us, receiving something that had nothing to do with our efforts is terrifying, because we've grown up being told that everything in life must come through a combination of blood, sweat, and tears. Except it's not actually true—it's just the place we grew comfortable in after learning how to get our lives together.

By allowing ourselves to receive our deepest desires as gift, we are therefore able to free ourselves from the life of striving that fills us with burnout and anxiety today and leads to a life far emptier than we expect. Instead, we can wear the easy yoke of God's

---

13. Titus 1:4 (MSG)

provision and care for our lives, leading to a life of fullness and sweetness today and more than our wildest dreams in the future.

Finally, by choosing a life of contentment and trust in God, we learn to be patient, as we cease chasing after the life we thought we wanted and allow God to seed our lives with gifts at the time of his choosing. A big motivating force behind striving is impatience. As we've discussed, we all have a laundry list of goals, dreams, ambitions, and desires that fuel us on a daily basis. But if you're like most people, you don't want to wait for the dream—you want it today. We may not say it out loud, but if we had to choose between waiting for whatever it is that we want, we'd take it today. And since most of us can't have it today, we settle for a sense of progress towards it each day and so expend a tremendous amount of energy on our pursuits so we can tell ourselves that we're a little bit closer to what we want when we fall asleep that night.

In the alternative of patience, we begin to see that the time that passes between the creation and fulfillment of desire is actually more valuable than whatever it is that we want to make happen for ourselves or receive freely. In waiting we see that, "What God does in us while we wait is as important as what it is we are waiting for . . . Waiting is not just something we have to do while we get what we want. It is part of the process of becoming what God wants us to be."[14]

Therefore we are free to not only rest in God's care and provision for us; we can take solace in the waiting, knowing that it's creating the transformation within us that we actually desire, while whatever external thing we hope for is on its way. And by taking this solace, we can turn off our frantic hyperactivity that we think is moving us forward but is actually sucking the life out of us while leading us to mirages. When we root our identity in our position as children of God, we no longer need our desires to be fulfilled but can simply receive what he desires to give us in the timing of his choosing.

It's important to note that when we resist waiting on God, we refuse his invitations to become like Christ. When we stay stuck

---

14. Ortberg, *If You Want to Walk on Water*, 178–79.

in striving, forcing our way to get what we want, we pay a price ourselves, as we avoid becoming who we were created to be and even worse, ask others to pay a price on our behalf when we abuse them in the pursuit of our own interests. When we focus on what we want and refuse to be patient, we end up settling for less than what God has for us. For all of us, our final destination is eternal, regardless of how fast we live life today. We can't speed up arriving at the character we need for our eternal home, but we can arrive for it better prepared if we learn contentment along the way. As Eugene Peterson writes, "How can I get them to see that I am working, right now, silently and invisibly, but surely and eternally, in their lives and in their history? How can I get them to see the connections between what they are doing now and who they will be in ten years, in twenty years?"[15]

While embracing contentment is key to our journey to reach our final home, it also has practical benefits in our present lives. Ironically, by ceasing from striving, practicing contentment, and learning patience, we actually can become far more effective and accomplished through our own efforts than we could have ever thought possible. How is this true, and what proof do I have? None other than Warren Buffett—arguably the greatest investor of all time.

As Warren Buffett describes it, the profession of investing is a lot like baseball. What he means by this analogy is that similar to how there are times to swing at a pitch that are more likely to result in a hit, there are also times to invest that are more likely to result in good returns. And the great thing about investing is that there's no downside to not swinging. "The trick in investing is just to sit there and watch pitch after pitch go by and wait for the one right in your sweet spot. And if people are yelling, 'Swing, you bum!,' ignore them."[16] And so it is with our own careers. More often than not, there are no downsides to letting bad opportunities pass us by or spending less time working on things that actually aren't moving us forward. Except for most of us, the way we live

15. Peterson, *Run with the Horses*, 72.
16. Elkins, "Warren Buffett Simplifies Investing with a Baseball Analogy."

doesn't reflect this belief. If anything, we've come to confuse our level of activity with the level of results we achieve, thereby reducing our so-called batting average as we convince ourselves that our striving is leading us to what we want. But if instead, we take on the practice of contentment, we become people who not only can recognize a great pitch when we see one, but we actually have the energy and resolve to swing for the fences when we see the right opportunity, thereby increasing our batting average. Yes, time is actually on our side, and we no longer need to keep swinging because of the external or internal voices telling us that we're a bum if we don't.

In many ways, the core of a striving mentality is a life of distraction. The busyness of striving leads us to lose sight of doing what really matters. In the words of Eric Hoffer, "The feeling of being hurried is not usually the result of living a full life and having no time. It is on the contrary, born of a vague fear that we are wasting our life. When we do not do the one thing we ought to do, we have no time for anything else, we are the busiest people in the world."[17] Rather than focus our lives on the unique life and calling that we've been gifted to receive from God, we settle for an endless chasing of the wind. We lack a sense of mission or clarity of vision that causes us to mistake our activity level for impact. Or as Henri Nouwen puts it, "The [social] compulsion manifests itself in the lurking fear of failing and the steady urge to prevent this by gathering more of the same—more work, more money, more friends."[18] By pursuing more of *everything*, we end making progress in *nothing*. A mirage of progress in a miasma of interests leads us to feeling stuck in the same place. In our hurry, we feel like we are moving forward, but we're just circling the spot we started in. The outcome of contentment is not inaction; rather it is conviction and clarity in calling. We cease trying to do all the things and instead put all of ourselves in the right things, and by not doing the right things, we reject the invitation to become what we were created to be.

---

17. Hoffer, *Reflections on the Human Condition*, 80.
18. Nouwen, *Spiritual Life*, 46.

The beauty of contentment is that while it feels like we are giving up a lot, we are actually receiving far more in return. But the counterintuitive reality is what makes moving from striving to contentment so difficult. Our process of growing up as adults teaches us that striving is the way life is supposed to be, and we are constantly inundated with messages that keep us from believing in that reality. Our instincts tell us that contentment is all loss, but we need to move forward in faith, believing that the reward is worth it. Our call is to accept the invitation of contentment to rejoice in all that you have and receive as gift the reality that God will give you far more you could ever imagine, without any effort of your choosing, while shaping you into something beautiful in the waiting, all while teaching you how to recognize the true life changing opportunities that come your way, and equipping you with the abilities to turn them into reality. The unquenched thirst of striving is apparent to everyone, so I hope you'll let go to receive contentment and the everlasting joy that comes along with it.

AUTHOR'S REFLECTION

Most of my work life to date has been characterized by projects or transactions. In other words, when something I've been working on is live, there is a high level of activity, due dates to keep in mind, and often a pervading sense of feeling behind. While this experience is often stressful, it's also energizing. Additionally, my responsibilities often have a clear sense of completion; when the deal closes, your work is done, so there's a tangible sense of "progress" to measure yourself by. As a result, I could (naively) measure how well I was moving towards my dreams and ambitions based on whether I had lots of projects on the go or had completed projects to point to as evidence that I was building the resume I needed to achieve whatever long-term career goal I had in mind at the time. In short, I was looking towards my level of activity and list of accomplishments as evidence that I was tracking to where I wanted to be in the future but failing to be fully attuned to the present.

The tension with this type of work emerges when the projects are completed or cancelled, and you suddenly find yourself with little to do. All of a sudden, that frenzy of activity is gone, as well as the sense of progress and accomplishment. Internally, I would start to ask myself, "If I'm not busy, how am I going to achieve the things I need to get promoted? Or how will prove that I'm capable of being the person I want to be in the future?"

In immaturity, my immediate reaction to fallow periods was to find ways to make myself busy again. A deep sense of discontent would rise up when things slowed down, pushing me to find ways to gain a sense of advancement once again. I would try and pick up projects from colleagues or help them with what they were working on or think of new initiatives that I could do, proving my capabilities. Ultimately, busyness and hurry were a distraction from the greater questions of whether I was becoming who God wanted me to be and whether I was following his path for my life.

Slowly, I'm beginning to see that these slow periods are actually blessings. With contentment in mind, quiet periods give me the time and space to reflect on what I've already received from God and enjoy these things fully as well. I have time to spend intentional time with my wife or friends. I can enjoy the fruits of my labor by savoring some of the things I like to do that are unconnected to performance. Most valuable of all, I can actually hear God. When all the hurry leaves my life, suddenly my body, soul, and mind are in a position to hear the still, small voice of God's spirit. I've slowed down enough to begin asking God questions about what he wants for my life and respond to the promptings of the Spirit, instead of mindlessly pursuing my own agenda. And it's in this space that God shows me the type of person he wants me to become and how he's using all of my daily experiences to shape me into his vision.

The foundation of my success is starting to invert. Instead of busyness and activity demonstrating the progress of my journey, the stillness is the sign I look for. These periods (whether brief or extended) are mountain top experiences that take stock of the journey to date in gratitude while pondering the next destination.

It's these periods of contentment where I'm reminded of all that God has done, while receiving new promises of what he will do and realizing that his plan is always more than the vain plans I had while clamoring through the thick forest of hurry.

DISCUSSION QUESTIONS

1. What are some examples of striving in your life?
2. Do you agree that contentment is a quality of life? Why or why not?
3. How do you react when hearing that God wants to give you your deepest desires without any merit on your part? Why do you think you reacted the way you did?
4. Why do we have a tendency to measure success by our "swings"? What can you stop doing to better prepare for your next home run pitch?

4

Capability to Vulnerability

How did you choose your career? If you're like me, at least part of the answer to that question is because you're good at some or many aspects of what you do on a daily basis while at work. This is self-evident to the point of being banal; no one pays anyone to do something they're bad at (at least to my knowledge!).

But how did you figure out what you're good at? Well again, if you're like me, there was likely some iterative process of experimentation with different hobbies, interests, and academics as you journeyed through the first couple decades of your life. This process is a key element of the struggle to "get our lives together." As we transition into adolescence, we go on a journey to discover what our skills and aptitudes are and then further these proficiencies to demonstrate a level of capability or mastery that could lead to self-sufficiency as an adult. As David Brooks summarizes this process, "If you go to the career-advice gurus to find your vocation, the question many will put at the center of your search is 'What is my talent?' One of the central preoccupations in the career-advice world is helping people identify strengths and then helping them figure out how to exploit them."[1] In short, we need to find a way to provide value beyond what we consume to become a net positive to the world we inhabit.

Did you notice what the main criteria for investing one's time in a skill or vocation tends to be? Typically, it's a natural inclination or ability in an area of expertise. Put another way, we tend to gravitate to what comes easy or naturally to us when we try something new. Now this inclination isn't inherently bad. In fact, when we're growing up and have a finite amount of time to discover a talent that can put a roof over our head and food on our table, focusing our efforts on our inherent abilities is a highly efficient way to reach the destination.

However, at a certain point, using capability as a primary decision criterion for how we make career decisions and decide how to invest our time begins to decline in usefulness. This decline is evident for several reasons.

For one, when we only spend our time doing things that we're good at, we risk becoming stale as our day-to-day descends into relative monotony and predictability that's best reserved for machines.

Additionally, we eventually master whatever we're proficient in. In the book *Outliers* by Malcolm Gladwell, he posited that it takes roughly ten thousand hours for an individual to master a skill.[2] The average person spends approximately two thousand hours per year at work, meaning that it takes roughly five years of full-time work to master a skill. Assuming the average person works for forty years of their life, that offers the possibility of mastering eight skills while on the job. One can only imagine how boring and lifeless work would become if we chose to focus on a handful of things we've already mastered for several decades, instead of trying something new.

Finally, a focus on capability ultimately leads us to seek comfort over growth. Once we reach a level of capability that vastly exceeds the average person, we are essentially immune from

1. Brooks, *Second Mountain*, 110–11.
2. Gladwell, *Outliers*, 35-68.

criticism or questioning, allowing us to inhabit a safe space that is free from any self-doubt about our ability to produce and therefore our insecurities and value as a person. As Lee Hardy says, "The ego wants you to choose a job and a life that you can use as a magic wand to impress others."[3] Frankly, many of us would rather stick to what we already know than expose ourselves to the risk of failing and looking foolish while trying something new, even if in the long-term it would bring us a greater sense of joy and satisfaction than continuing to do the same thing over and over.

There is also an irony in choosing to limit ourselves to what we're capable of, as it leads us to stay stuck where we are. Our assumption is that if we focus on what we're best at and hone our craft, once we get good enough in whatever we've specialized in, that expertise is what will propel us to the next level, whether that's a promotion, changing companies, or otherwise. The reality is often the opposite of that. In fact, so many times, the next step on the career ladder requires embracing an entirely new set of skills, many of which are unrelated to the skills an individual learned and gained proficiency in up until that point.

Nancy Duarte talks about the professional transition from "explorer" to "explainer,"[4] a step that many junior employees need to make as they progress to mid-level roles in their careers. In this transition, explorers, people tasked with going deep in the details, particularly the quantitative, must learn how to explain what the data means to other team members. As people make this transition, they go from being individual contributors to strategy advisors. But note, the skill that makes them a strategic advisor, namely storytelling, is not the same skill they had previously—in this case, attention to detail. And so it goes in other regards. A very common transition that many struggle with is going from individual contributor to team leader, from working *for* people to working *through* people. Skills as an individual contributor, especially technical ones such as financial analysis, legal drafting, graphic design,

---

3. Brooks, *Second Mountain*, 43.
4. Duarte, *Data Story*, 8.

or otherwise, give way to people management, motivation, delegation, and project management.

Beyond the practical considerations, there are spiritual implications to a reliance on capability as a guide for our work lives as well. In particular, when we choose to focus on capability in our careers we end up removing any need to rely on something greater than ourselves, especially God.

Wait, aren't we all supposed to use the skills and abilities that God gave us to meet our needs and be a blessing to others? Yes, absolutely. We've all been gifted in unique ways, and it's a tragedy whenever someone chooses to squander their gifts. We even see individuals in Exodus gifted in specific ways and empowered with the Spirit to build God's tabernacle in partnership with him.[5] Capability is not inherently bad, but it needs to exist in the right order of emphasis in our lives.

But for many people, their gifts end up being ends to themselves or vehicles that they can rely on to provide the life that they want, including safety, security, provision, and identity, with the effect of eliminating our reliance on God. Bob Buford describes his experience this way: "The business arena was the venture where I proved myself—my worth, my wisdom—each day; it was a stage on which I could demonstrate my gifts and my savvy. It was a comfortable world for me, not merely because it was familiar . . . It was measurable."[6] What was meant to be a gift that would create a greater depth of relationship with God as we co-created in partnership ends up being an idol that leads to self-sufficient isolation. We have lost sight of the fact that our faith "snatches us away from ourselves and places us outside ourselves, so that we do not depend on our own strength, conscience, experience, person, or works but depend on that which is outside ourselves, that is, on the promise and truth of God, which cannot deceive."[7]

The irony in much of this is that we crave the transcendent in our work. We deeply desire to experience God in our workplace

---

5. Exod 31:1–11 (NIV)
6. Buford, *Halftime*, 50.
7. Sittser, *Water from a Deep Well*, 217.

and to see his mighty arm in the places we spend most of our days, but our actual lives are more like that of teenage kids telling their parents to leave them alone to do what they want as a demonstration of their independence. This reality echoes the observation that "much of what we do in the first half is not imbued with the presence of the eternal."[8] In our work lives, God is like the parent of those teenagers: he knows when he's not wanted as we demonstrate our independence through the capability of our vocational lives and refuse to allow ourselves to experience any dependence on him in the workplace. As Paul writes, "My grace is sufficient for you, for my power is made perfect in weakness."[9] Reality suggests that the majority of us are running in the opposite direction of where Paul says we'll encounter God when it comes to our careers.

However, while the practical and spiritual elements of prioritizing capability are now evident, the most destructive element of the overemphasis is that it's a denial of reality. What do I mean by this?

For starters, when we cling to our own capability and find meaning, significance, and affirmation because of what we can do, what began as a healthy confidence and self-regard becomes pride as we feel a sense of superiority for being capable of performing tasks that others are incapable of. However, this pride is ultimately blinding, because in focusing on what others cannot do, we lose sight of what we are not able to do or convince ourselves we are capable of everything when that is not the case. Additionally, we can avoid accountability, as an excessive focus on our capability can prevent us from acknowledging our failures and mistakes. By refusing to acknowledge the reality that we have limits and are fallible, we are buying into what Parker Palmer calls "the myth of the limitless self"[10] instead of acknowledging our limitations and experiencing the joy and freedom that comes from doing so.

Further, we have all been wounded, hurt, or experienced failure at some point in our lives. For many of us, these experiences have come while at the workplace. We've been demeaned by

---

8. Buford, *Halftime*, 85.
9. 2 Cor 12:9 (NIV)
10. Palmer, *Let Your Life Speak*, 39.

a colleague or manager, we made a mistake that negatively affected our credibility, we've had lapses in our ethical judgement, or we've even done the right thing and been reprimanded for it. All of these situations and others are painful. They are painful to the point that we'd rather ignore that pain and instead cling to the false sense of goodness and worth that comes from relying on our capability.

However, our tendency to rely on our capability to provide a sense of self-esteem simply serves as façade to cover up our underlying sense of insecurity that has arisen from the pain we've experienced at work or outside of work. This pain is so acute for many that we'd rather live in an imaginary world filled with our success and accomplishments—because we are more comfortable with what they say about us—than deal with the narratives we've come to believe because of the wounds we carry with us. This is a key factor as to why so many successful, ambitious people experience what psychologists call imposter syndrome, which is marked by devoting an excessive amount of effort to hide inadequacies from other people;[11] nowhere is this dynamic more at play than in the workplace! This leaves many trying unsuccessfully to drum up a sense of worthiness from their competencies.

If imposter syndrome is so pervasive, and relying on what we're good at won't salve the pain we're experiencing, then why does everyone keep doing it? A big part of the answer to this question is that societally, and particularly in the workplace, we don't value this type of pain. We value the type of pain we're in control of, like when people put in long hours to start a business or train for a professional sport. But when pain comes from something we didn't choose? We go straight to putting our head in the sand, practically speaking. It's precisely because we don't value the pain from our wounds, hurts, and failures that we see these experiences solely as reminders of when we didn't accomplish what we set out for or experienced a deep hit to our self-worth. As a result, capability becomes our protective mechanism that we use to prove to ourselves that we're good enough and don't ever have to risk being hurt again.

---

11. Ortberg, *If You Want to Walk on Water*, 63.

But what if that pain was meaningful? What if that pain had eternal significance? What if the most valuable experiences in our careers were what went wrong and how those experiences made us like Christ? What if God actually wanted to use our vulnerability and failures to heal us and in turn the world? As Tyler Staton writes, "It is not by our gifts, insights, ideas, or qualifications that God is determined to heal the world, but by our scars. By his wounds we are healed, and by our wounds the healing is shared."[12] However, if we want God to heal our wounds we first need to embrace them instead of avoiding them. As noted earlier, capability for many of us becomes a protective mechanism that we use to shield us from experiencing the same pain again. There is a psychotherapy model known as Internal Family Systems (IFS) that captures this behavior well.

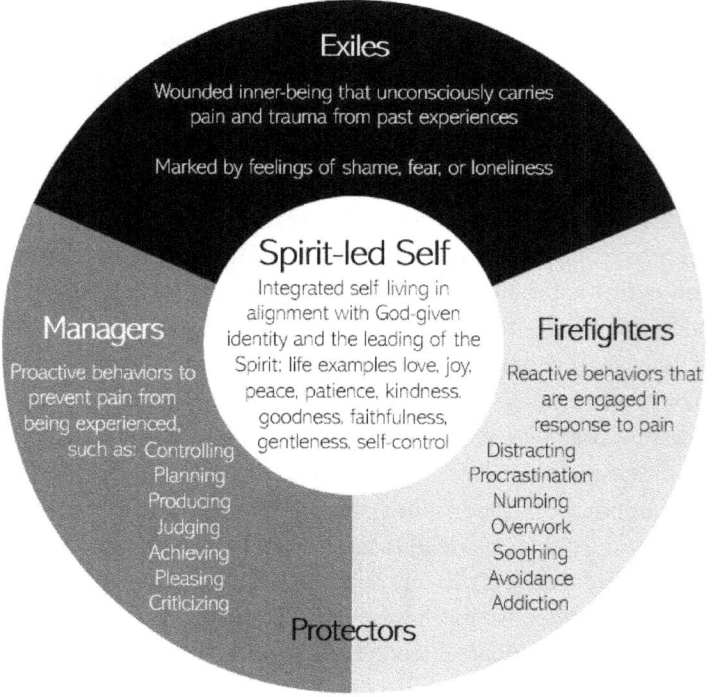

12. Staton, *Praying Like Monks*, 86.

Using this model, we can see that capability closely aligns with the manager behaviors in the model. This is the part of us that wants to control, plan, judge, achieve, and please others or express criticism, all in the hope of never experiencing pain again. In more unhealthy situations, we also see capability show up as a firefighter, as we turn to overwork and excessive ambition to distract us from the pain bubbling up inside of us. In the worst forms of this behavior, we can find ourselves filled with anger and rage or completely dissociated from work because of traumatic experiences in our workplace or otherwise. Lastly, we have the part of the self we refer to as the exile, or the root of our pain. This is the part of us that has been deeply wounded and therefore carries a great sense of pain wherever we go, until it's been healed. This is the part that many of us are blind to, and subsequently the piece of us that so many unconsciously ignore as they express manager and firefighter behaviors that are often celebrated and praised in the workplace. But if these behaviors are praised in the workplace and can help me get ahead, why do we need to heal these parts of ourselves?

Because if we don't bring healing to our exiles, we will work out of a position that seeks to compensate for that pain with a solution that is entirely unsuitable for healing it. Just ask any successful athlete, actor, or businessperson whether their success changed how they felt inside; the resounding experience of anyone who achieved their goals is that it only felt empty and created despair over the fact that fulfilling their ambitions changed absolutely nothing about how they felt. Matthew Perry, star of *Friends*, one of the most popular TV shows of all time said it this way: "There was steam coming out of my ears, I wanted to be famous so badly. You want the attention, you want the bucks, and you want the best seat in the restaurant. I didn't think what the repercussions would be . . .When [becoming successful] happens, it's kind of like Disneyland for a while," Mr. Perry says of hitting it big after *Friends* started in 1994. "For me it lasted about eight months, this feeling of 'I've made it, I'm thrilled, there's no problem in the world.' And then you realize that it doesn't accomplish anything, it's certainly not filling any holes in your life." Perry goes on to say, "I needed to succeed at whatever I was doing so I could feel better about myself."[13] In other words, a quintessential example of working out of the illusion of capability to avoid the pain carried deep inside.

What's more, if we don't acknowledge and bring healing to our exiles, we remain blind to our true self, or the spirit-led self. Deep down, this is who we were created to be: people filled with love, joy, peace, kindness, goodness, faithfulness, gentleness, and self-control. People filled with calmness, compassion, creativity, clarity, curiosity, confidence and courage as they invest their talent and energy into the work they have been called to. It's this part of us that we need to bring to the surface so that we can discover the work that we were made for, and complete in accordance with our giftings. It's this part of us that can accept failures and learn the lessons we need to learn to move forward. It's this part of us that God wants us to bring into the workplace to co-create in the renewal of all things. But we can only discover this self if we seek to unravel the managers, firefighters, and exiles that obscure our true being. And to unravel these pieces of us means we need to go to where it hurts the most, acknowledge the reality of that pain and bring it to God for healing, instead of trying to fill that void with empty victories. We can reject the world's message that maturity is based on independence and strength and see the reality that maturity is the acceptance of our weakness and dependance on God's strength. In summarizing Fred Rogers' life, David Brooks writes, "Usually adulthood is about moving to assertiveness and self-sufficiency. But Rogers moved toward vulnerability and dependence . . . Where there's humility there is majesty; where there's weakness, there's might; where there's death, there's life."[14]

As we begin to discover who we were actually created to be, we can then be liberated to see not only what we were truly gifted at (instead of what we get praised for, or can make a lot of money from) but the true work that God has invited us to participate in. Or perhaps even most aligned with the heart of God, we can work to ensure that the pain we felt will never be felt by those around

---

13. Kennedy, "Fame He Craved Came, but It Wasn't Enough."
14. Brooks, *Second Mountain*, 260–61.

us. As Paul writes, "I know how to be brought low, and I know how to abound. In any and every circumstance, I have learned the secret of facing plenty and hunger, abundance and need. I can do all things through him who strengthens me."[15] Here we see the complement of capability and vulnerability: whether in strength or weakness, Paul is able to abound because of his dependence on God who does the strengthening. In other words, "Weakness carries within it a secret power. The care and the trust that flow from weaknesses can open up the heart. The one who is weaker can call forth powers of life in the one who is stronger."[16]

As an aside, it's important to acknowledge that for some readers, your starting place might be vulnerability; for whatever reason, you have never felt empowered to go out and co-create with God. Hopefully this invitation of embracing your vulnerability can be the impetus to see how God wants to use you in the workplace in an entirely new way while also giving you the courage to discover what you are uniquely capable of accomplishing in your work.

Assuming we are able to break free of the bonds of capability that keep us from attaining the work life that we truly desire, can we then go on to live out our truest self without any hint of resistance or future pain in our work lives? Unfortunately not, but we will be able to welcome it from a completely different posture. In fact, we should not even be surprised when we encounter pain in the workplace. As the apostle Peter writes, "If when you do good and suffer for it you endure, this is a gracious thing in the sight of God. For to this you have been called, because Christ also suffered for you, leaving you an example, so that you might follow in his steps."[17] If anything, when we are working out of our Spirit-led self, or doing good as Scripture phrases it, it is a *gracious* thing that we should experience this as we get to live out the example of Christ's own life and so become more like him. And as we are transformed into the image of Christ through our experience in the workplace,

---

15. Phil 4:12–13 (ESV)
16. Brooks, *Second Mountain*, 223.
17. 1 Pet 2:20–21 (ESV)

we gain eternal significance as we are increasingly prepared for a life with God in the flesh.

The value of workplace suffering is not only limited to the next life either. Our suffering can actually bring redemption to our vocational lives, and therefore the world. But how? Allow me to explain. As we've discussed, many of us land in professional circumstances where we have experienced pain as a result of wounds, hurt, trauma, or failures. This sensation of pain runs deep into our bones as we cry out at the injustice of it, knowing that this is not how the world should be, yet feeling the disconnect that this what our reality is. Feeling this injustice, usually our default position, and also the world's position, is to fix the injustice on our own terms. We seek to right the wrong, say, by returning a condemning word back to a coworker or trying to find retribution through an HR department. This reflects our: "instinct . . . to drum up [our] own lovableness, to become lovable in some way you can define and control, to try to become in [our] own eyes what [we] already are in God's."[18]

This instinct doesn't solve anything though. We may feel better because "justice" has been served by our definition of it, but sadly the world remains in the same cycle of perpetual injustice as we consciously or unconsciously act out of our manager and firefighter selves. The invitation of Jesus in these circumstances is to turn the other cheek, like he did. Our invitation to bring true renewal to our workplaces is to "take away the tensions and sins of the [workplace] by absorbing them, carrying them, transforming them, and not giving them back in kind." We can then become like Jesus who "*resisted the instinct to give back in kind, hatred for hatred, curses for curses, jealousy for jealousy, murder for murder.*" Who "held and transformed these things rather than simply retransmitting them." Who "took away the sins of the world by absorbing them, at great cost to himself."[19] Simply put, we are more willing to forgive the brokenness of our colleagues when we come to accept our own brokenness.

18. Staton, *Praying Like Monks*, 77.
19. Rolheiser, *Sacred Fire*, 160–61.

Our craving for the transcendent in the workplace will not come from another invention, another wildly successful company going public, or even a tremendous amount of money given to charity. It will come when the unending cycle of evil, hatred, greed, jealousy, and selfish ambition is gradually rooted out of the workplace by a community of Christians absorbing that sin and only giving back love in return, until our workplaces come to reflect the love, joy, and peace that we've been promised by Jesus if we follow his way. We cannot do this through our own efforts; there is not enough raw human talent to accomplish this. To live this way is only possible by depending on God himself and being filled with his Spirit. Our best hope is to pray as Susanna Wesley did: "Help me, O Lord, to make a true use of all disappointments and calamities in this life, in such wise that they may unite my heart more closely with Thee. Cause them to separate my affections from worldly things and inspire my soul with more vigor in the pursuit of true happiness."[20]

AUTHOR'S REFLECTION

Growing up, I experienced a lack of positive affirmation from my parents, peers, and other influences in my life. It wasn't until I began to reflect on my own life and how I experienced the workplace during the early phase of my career that I realized how much this lack of affirmation had become a weight on me. I was desperate to prove my capability in the performance-based environments of the workplace. If I did a good job, I was elated, but receiving criticism, even if it was well-meaning, was a burden that my wounded soul couldn't bear. Often, I would be filled with bitterness and resentment towards the person criticizing my work and revert to a position of defensiveness that squashed debate and prevented me from learning or receiving good instruction. To avoid the pain, I would work even harder to do a more "perfect" job, but this was

---

20. Owens, "Susanna Wesley on Prayer."

always to no avail, because as a human, I will always make mistakes no matter how hard I try.

My desire to prove my capability existed not only on a micro level, but on a macro level as well. I grew up in a small town, went to a university that was not well-regarded, and graduated from a business program that lacked the prestige of other programs in the region. As a result, I always viewed my relative career position as inferior to anyone that graduated from more well-regarded universities or worked at prominent companies. Naively, my planned solution was to overcome the humble origins of my education and professional background and attend a highly ranked graduate business program. I thought that if I didn't have the cachet early in my career, I could get it later on, thereby proving my capability in the "big leagues" and thereby addressing any felt disappointment from my career success to that point.

In other words, whether in the workplace or in my long-term ambitions, I was walking with a limp that I was trying (unsuccessfully) to compensate for with performance and external evidence of my capability. Fortunately, God didn't allow me to settle for idols that weren't going to satisfy the way that I hoped that they would. I never got into any of the MBA programs I applied to, despite having the experience and academic performance to. And when I tried to move to New York to work in the upper levels of finance, God shut those doors too.

As I began to reflect on what appeared to be failures in my career, the Holy Spirit shone a light that highlighted the brokenness of my motives behind these now unfulfilled ambitions. At the same time, God also began revealing deeper elements of my being that had remain dormant and that he wanted to use. People close to me began pointing out that I had a natural gift for writing and expressing my thoughts, so I began stepping out in that talent, including this book. Others noted that I had the spiritual gift of teaching, something that I had never even considered and frankly would have been too afraid to step into. In his mercy, God led me to a deeper understanding of the capability he created me with, instead of trying to prove a false sense of capability based on the world's standards. And through the vulnerability of failing at something I had earnestly pursued with my own efforts, he has used the circumstances to fill me with a voice that desires to encourage and strengthen other believers in the workplace to pursue their own journey of maturity of the workplace and step into God's deeper callings in their lives.

DISCUSSION QUESTIONS

1. Do you currently feel stuck in your career? How might this experience relate to the concept of capability?
2. Do you believe you're avoiding God by using your natural gifts? Why or why not?
3. What are some of your protective behaviors at work?
4. Do you agree that forgiveness is the most powerful force for transformation in our workplaces? How could it change work in your context?

5

Scarcity to Abundance

"Every time a friend succeeds, I die a little."
—Gore Vidal

How many people resonate with Gore Vidal's quote on a deep level? Be honest with yourself; you likely don't want to admit it because you know this sort of mindset isn't the way life's supposed to be lived, but deep down we all know that's how many of us feel. Just think about some examples of your own life: the friend with the bigger home, the one that just sold the company they founded, your cousin who travels the world for work, your university roommate that got promoted to partner before age thirty-five. Examples abound of the people that are crushing it for everyone to see while inspiring jealousy and insecurity in the rest of us. Even when those people are our colleagues, friends, neighbors, classmates, or perhaps just someone you see on social media or in the news.

Whether we know it or not, this insecurity is an anchor that we all carry with us from our childhood. At the root of our existence as humans is the need to be relationally known and for our physical needs to be met. However, given the finite nature of humans and the imperfection of our world, at some point, every child will experience their needs not being met in the moment. The tragedy of these needs not being met isn't limited to the direct emotional or physical consequences however. Beyond these emotional and physical needs is the core desire to be loved, and in our immaturity as children, we conflate our emotional and physical needs with our soul-level desire to be loved unconditionally. We thus unknowingly come to assume that the satisfaction of our emotional and material needs are the proof of being loved and therefore conclude that if our emotional and physical needs are not met, we are not loved.

It is at this point that the false self of every person is born. As Brennan Manning writes, "The false self was born when as children we were not loved well or were rejected or abandoned." This false self is "preoccupied with acceptance and approval," has an "insatiable appetite for affirmation," "demands to be noticed," and "buys [into] outside experiences to furnish a personal source of meaning" where "the pursuit of money, power, glamour, sexual prowess, recognition and status enhances one's self importance and creates the illusion of success."[1]

The false self mistakenly assumes that anything tangentially related to being known by other people will satisfy their emotional need and that anything that can be done to avoid unfulfilled physical needs is worthwhile. These double-edged pursuits thus come to serve as false proofs of being loved. In other words, "We were all missing something as children, and as adults we're willing to put up with a lot in order to get it."[2] Thus, our false self creates a protective mechanism whereby performance and possessions become the substitute for relational intimacy that we all desire. So long as we perform and protect ourselves, we can know that we are safe and secure, regardless of the circumstances.

---

1. Manning, *Abba's Child*, 16.
2. Brooks, *Second Mountain*, 95.

Unfortunately, these pursuits don't work. No amount of attention, praise, material possessions, or money can meet our emotional needs or desires for security and therefore can't satisfy our heart's longing to be loved. So, while in immaturity, we attempt to fix the ache in our souls through our own efforts, we are never satisfied with the results. When we do not believe that we are loved, we are faced with a soul-level void that can never be filled, leading to the conclusion that only an unending supply of acclaim or an infinite pool of money will give us the feeling our soul demands.

The reality is that there is only a finite amount of other people's attention and a fixed amount of resources when we look at the world from a naturalistic perspective. Realizing that our world has a finite amount of resources lands heavily on a heart searching to be known and loved by the infinite. This juxtaposition of infinite desire and finite resources creates an anxiety-inducing tension within us known as a scarcity mindset, as our pursuit of limited external sources of validation and security increasingly grate against our unsatisfied longings for love. We consciously or unconsciously come to see that our infinite desire will not be satisfied by the limited praise or possessions that we already have, and mistakenly conclude that an infinite supply of either will. We thus journey out into life seeking the satisfaction of the infinite through our own efforts and see everyone else as a competitive claim to our unmet desires. We operate out of what David Brooks calls a "warrior mentality" where "life is a battle for scarce resources and it's always us versus them, zero-sum. The ends justify the means."[3] Simply put, if we have a desire for something infinite and we can only see finite resources, any subtraction of the finite by someone else will subtract from us. As a result, we often believe that when our so-called competition receives what we're looking for, it detracts from the satisfaction of our own desires as well, leading to a zero-sum competitive environment between us and everyone else.

In our work lives, this scarcity mindset has two specific applications.

---

3. Brooks, *Second Mountain*, 35.

First, we look to performance-based praise and affirmation from other people to satisfy our emotional needs of being known and loved. As noted previously, the false self is preoccupied with acceptance and approval, which is a direct response to an unmet need to be emotionally seen and known at some point in an individual's life. For many, the false self is the dominant mode of living during the immature phase of our careers: "people climbing the first mountain spend a lot of time thinking about reputation management. They are always keeping score."[4] Put another way, we tell ourselves that if other people can't be relied upon to know us as we desire to be known, we will live our lives to guarantee that other people notice us and regard us as we want to be known.

We then carry this part of ourselves into our workplaces, where we continue the futile exercise of trying to address our unmet emotional needs through achievements, titles, money, promotions, and the praise of other people. Many of us get what we're chasing after too, but it never really satisfies the way that we hoped. When our inability to meet our own needs through our own efforts becomes more pronounced, we experience an ache of dissatisfaction. Because of this, we cease to be content with the payoff of what our own performance produces. This realization, combined with our view that life is competitive and zero sum, leads us to feel threatened by what is happening to the people around us.

Left unchecked, we come to perceive everything as a threat to our own needs being met. Whenever someone gets promoted or succeeds, buys something we want, or is better at something than we are, we feel jealousy and unhappiness. As Pete Scazzero writes, we become guilty of "spiritual envy: feeling unhappy when others do well spiritually, [and] always comparing."[5] Even worse than feelings of jealousy or unhappiness is the active sabotage of other people's success. As Eugene Peterson puts it, this approach is like "a sniping pettiness that wants to cut people down to our size so that we will not be embarrassed in our own littleness."[6] This is

---

4. Brooks, *Second Mountain*, xii.
5. Scazzero, *Emotionally Healthy Spirituality*, 104.
6. Peterson, *Running with the Horses*, 92.

the aspect of ourselves that is so focused on the unmet needs of the false self that we mistakenly believe that others receiving the false substitutes of relational intimacy somehow prevents us from attaining what we truly want as well. Many may know of extreme examples of this type of behavior; talking about our own achievements and successes whenever someone shares their own, criticizing someone after they've been promoted or achieved a goal, or perhaps even getting in the way of someone trying to achieve something. But it can be more subtle too, like refusing to praise someone for good work because of the insecurity it produces in us.

However, whether it's the mistaken pursuit of gratifying the false self with empty pursuits, holding others we perceive as better than us in contempt, or actively trying to destroy the efforts of those around us, we all live life from a sense of scarcity; our unmet emotional need to be seen and known as a child haunts us in the present, as we attempt to meet that need through our own efforts, distract ourselves from the hurt with pangs of jealousy, or take from others to compensate for what we feel we're lacking.

Second, we try to guarantee safety and security by storing up material possessions and wealth to guard against the risk of our material needs not being met by forces outside of our control. Whether we know it or not, we have all experienced material lack at some point in our lives. For some, this reflected true poverty: going without food or shelter, lacking clothes, or a dearth of play. For others, this was unmet aspirations: not getting the toy we wanted, someone having a better bike than we did, or having the friend that always had the cool new thing while we had to make do with what we have. Or perhaps circumstances in life meant that we went from having a lot of things to much less than before. The common thread is a felt sense of physical need or want being unsatisfied.

Irrespective of the specific example, the unsatisfied material need also gives rise to the false self. This version of the false self (rightly or wrongly) comes to believe that material needs are equivalent to being loved and that any experienced shortfall in need or want is equivalent to not being loved. The false self therefore enters the world and workplace seeking to ensure that they will never go without again or react with hostility to any perceived threat to what they have or aspire to. We become like the woman at the well in John 4:7 who, "like many of us today, exists within a separation worldview, sourced in scarcity, and thereby committed to a life of self-protection."[7]

An easy example of this is the individual that never seems to stop saving money. They have a great job, a home, and ample savings for retirement but can somehow never find money to enjoy life with or give away to those in need. Ironically, this type of behavior is praised by most; we seem to love the ability to pinch pennies, even if it's a pointless exercise in the grand scheme of things. For this person, no amount of saving is ever enough because the perceived risk of losing it all will always drive their decisions. Jesus himself rebukes this behavior in the parable of the old fool, as the building of bigger barns to store up for oneself is contrary to being rich toward God.[8]

Similar to the person who can't stop saving money is the person who has no time available for anyone other than themselves. Whenever there is an opportunity to serve others, or invest time in other people, this person will always say no because they just don't have enough time. But the reason they don't have enough time is because they've jam packed their life full of things to ensure that they get what they think they need. Any time given up simply subtracts from this person's ability to attain what they're striving for.

We can see the reverse of the two previous examples in the flippant spender that always has new clothes, vehicles, homes, vacations, or otherwise. Despite having a well-paid job, they are chronically in debt because buying things equates to the sense of being loved, and no amount of purchases will fulfill the soul-level desire to be known as the beloved.

Finally, we can see the vain efforts of both the security- or pleasure-oriented person produce unnecessary conflict when they interact in the workplace and beyond. They will feel intense resentment or jealousy when someone else has something that they

---

7. Winship, *Living Fearless*, 107.
8. Luke 12:16–21 (NIV)

don't have or simply draws the attention of other people away from them. They will hold on to well-paying jobs far past the point of having provided for their own needs to the detriment of others further behind them in maturity. They will react viciously to anyone who is perceived as a threat to their income or possessions.

Within all of these cases and more, we see people incorrectly believing that past unmet needs have equated to a lack of being loved and concluding that the answer to being loved is through money and possessions. But given an infinite desire for love, no amount of possessions or financial assets will ever satisfy, and the things that others have will always feel like a subtraction from what we have.

This mindset of scarcity is so often at the root of an inability to be generous. Even when the basic needs of so many have been met for many lives over, the desire to guarantee security and find satisfaction through more of everything prevents us from giving freely of our time or money to those who truly are in need. As Ronald Rolheiser describes this scarcity mentality, "If we breathe out a sense of scarcity that makes us calculate and be fearful, then calculation and fearfulness will be the air we reinhale."[9] Indeed, the power of the false self is so strong that in our quest to prove to ourselves that we're loved because of what we own or can count, we end up cutting ourselves off from the people around us, further exacerbating the sense of being known and loved by others. As John Maxwell writes, "When you choose to hoard what you have, rather than give, you become the center of your own lonely universe and you become less content, not more. As a result, you repel both people and potential blessings."[10]

Now that we've fleshed out what a scarcity mindset looks like in practical terms, it's important to go further and observe that when we understand life to be full of scarcity because of our past unmet needs and respond by putting ourselves in the position of responsibility, we're not actually free individuals, as we are guided by our reactions instead of true free will. Further, this reactivity

---

9. Rolheiser, *Sacred Fire*, 279.
10. Maxwell, *How Successful People Grow*, 133.

is ultimately futile, as our desire to be loved is not in our power to attain. As we live a life of scarcity, where we continue to seek validation from other people and material goods to compensate for our unmet emotional and physical needs, we unfortunately become blind to our true need and calling, which is to be known as beloved by God.

When we step into our true calling of beloved by God, we "define [ourselves] radically as one beloved by God; [where] God's love for you and his choice of you constitute [our] worth" and where we let that reality "become the most important thing in [our] lives." As we define ourselves as beloved by God, we can increasingly say that "the basis of my personal worth is not my possessions, my talents, not esteem of others, reputation . . . not kudos of appreciation from parents and kids, not applause, and everyone telling you how important you are to the place . . . I stand anchored now in God before whom I stand naked, this God who tells me, 'You are my son, my beloved one.'"[11]

To escape a life characterized by scarcity, we must start with understanding our position as beloved by God, as this is the only source of fulfillment that will allow us to escape the felt sense of deficit we carry that propels us outward in pursuit of fame, success, achievements, money, and power. It's only by understanding the unchanging nature of God's affection towards us that we can relinquish the ever-changing attachments that never satisfy and strain relationships with those around us. Without an identity, as the beloved, we will stay stuck in the hamster wheel.

Staying stuck chasing after these external markers of success, meaning, and security doesn't just harm ourselves either. When our lives our dominated by scarcity, we also unwittingly accept and promote the world's definition of success and happiness as well, detracting from the truth of the gospel. So often we confuse what's popular with what leads to life. As Eugene Peterson writes, "Pliny the Elder once said that the Romans, when they couldn't make a building beautiful, made it big. The practice continues to be popular: If we can't do it well, we make it larger. We add dollars

---

11. Manning, *Abba's Child*, 33.

to our income, rooms to our houses, activities to our schedules, appointments to our calendars. And the quality of life diminishes with each addition. On the other hand, every time that we retrieve part of our life from the crowd and respond to God's call to us, we are that much more ourselves, more human. Every time we reject the habits of the crowd and practice the disciplines of faith, we become a little more alive."[12]

The consequences of settling for what the world promotes in the workplace aren't limited to our own lives either. When we accept a belief that satisfaction comes from a limited menu of advancement and material goods, we are by default pitted against each other in a winner-take-all battle for the same things, leading to the underlying resentment and outward sabotage that so often comes with a competitive dynamic. In the Epistle of James it says, "For where jealousy and selfish ambition exist, there will be disorder and every vile practice,"[13] perfectly encapsulating the environments that we experience in the workplace that lead to so much unhappiness. In short, we cannot all attain the limited substitutes for happiness that the world promotes through natural effort.

The antidote to the competitive rat race, as already mentioned, is accepting the invitation of our true calling as the beloved of God. Importantly, this calling is distinct to the false callings of the world in that this calling is available to everyone without compromise to anyone else. This general calling aligns with Jesus' own life, as God declared Jesus as his beloved Son, before Jesus performed any of the work that formed his ministry.[14] Just like Jesus, receiving our general calling to be known as the beloved in turn positions us to receive our unique calling from God. As Eugene Peterson writes, "There is no human being who is not useful with a part to play in what God is doing. And there is no human being who is not unique with special lines and colors and forms distinct from anyone else."[15]

12. Peterson, *Run with the Horses*, 139.
13. Jas 3:16 (ESV)
14. Matt 3:17 (NIV)
15. Peterson, *Run with the Horses*, 75.

It's only when we're set free from pursuing the world's definition of success that we can receive a calling that's unconnected from these definitions. It's only when we've let go of trying to achieve what everyone else is trying to achieve that we can accept a calling that only we can achieve in partnership with God. If we're willing to accept this invitation to a unique calling, we are then able to see that our journey will have no comparison to anyone else's, and therefore we have no need to compare the fruits of our calling with those of another. Instead, all we will need to focus on is whether we're moving forward in our own journey or not. We can trust God to do the promoting in our lives, where advancement in the eyes of the world is his responsibility, not ours.

The measure of progress in our journey will be unlike how we've measured progress in the past, however. Where before we looked to external markers of success, like titles, possessions, and wealth, the primary markers now will be internal. Of these markers, a primary measurement will be the extent to which we truly believe in our position as the beloved, instead of our attempts to prove value to ourselves. It will also be measured by our ordinariness, which is simply "becoming so simply and naturally [ourselves] . . . the measures of what [we] might be if society did not distort [us] with greed or ambition or lust or desperate want."[16] And much of our progress will be demonstrated by "what we do in secret"[17] and framing what we do now in the perspective of how it is shaping us into the image of Christ.

When we arrive at the posture of knowing that we are *truly* the beloved of God, we in turn can believe that all of our deepest needs have been met by him. We can know without a shadow of a doubt that we are deeply loved by him, and this love is unconditional and entirely without merit. It's a love that's unconnected with anything we do, achieve, say, own, or think. It's a love that promises to take care of us no matter what happens in life. Paul reminds us that "it's important that you not misinterpret yourselves as people who are bringing this goodness to God. No, God brings it all to

16. Manning, *Abba's Child*, 32.
17. Peterson, *Run with the Horses*, 103.

you. *The only accurate way to understand ourselves is by what God is and by what he does for us*, not by what we are and what we do for him."[18] Whether we are at the zenith of wealth or struggling for our daily bread and everything in between, we can trust and rely on a God that has promised to meet our every need and more. We can now live out of the reality that we are safe and secure in the providential arms of God, irrespective of circumstances. We see this reality evidenced in Paul's prayer for the Ephesians: "For this reason I bow my knees before the Father, from whom every family in heaven and on earth is named, that according to the riches of his glory he may grant you to be strengthened with power through his Spirit in your inner being, so that Christ may dwell in your hearts through faith—that you, being rooted and grounded in love, may have strength to comprehend with all the saints what is the breadth and length and height and depth, and to know the love of Christ that surpasses knowledge, that you may be filled with all the fullness of God."[19]

When we understand our position as the beloved of God, we are transformed to understand that life is lived in abundance and not the scarcity we had previously understood. Further, as we come to know the reality of God's affection toward us and accept our unique calling, we fall out of the competitive, zero-sum dynamic that had pitted us against our colleagues, friends, neighbors and family. Instead, we are able to journey outwards and celebrate the victories and accomplishments of those around us. We are able to "rejoice with those who rejoice."[20]

By rejoicing in the success of other people, we begin to see that we can multiply the blessing that someone else has received. No longer are the accomplishments of others subtracting from our lives, but the reverse is true: we are far more known and loved by other people when we magnify them in their time of blessing. And by participating in the blessing that God is bestowing on others, we understand the true abundance of God and his gifts, as the

18. Rom 12:3 (MSG)
19. Eph 3:14-19 (ESV)
20. Rom 12:15 (NIV)

demonstration of our love towards others flows back to us as we become known as the people that build people up in their successes. This is the abundance of God: that the blessing of someone else becomes a blessing to us when we rightly rejoice in the good fortune of others. As John Maxwell puts it, "When you focus more on the wants and needs of others, more of your own wants and needs are met." As we do this, we become like "a river [that] flows, whatever water it receives, it gives away," but to become a river "requires an abundance mind-set—a belief that we will keep receiving."[21]

Similarly, when we come to understand the depth of God's promises to meet our needs, we are able to embrace true generosity with those around us. Not only are we able to give freely of our finances to those in need, we can pour out our blessing and support to help others achieve their goals and ambitions. We no longer need to worry whether helping someone will result in them getting a promotion that we want or having a business become more successful than our own efforts, as we know that our needs are fully and truly met for our own calling. We are free to give, bless, and empower everyone to achieve the calling that God has for them.

As we live out the invitations of an abundant life, we come to see that we are *all* sons and daughters of the kingdom of God. Our positions are irrespective of merit and granted to us out of the infinite love of God. We see this reality described in the story of Joseph, where the psalmist writes that he was made lord of the king's house and ruler of his possessions.[22] We see this again as Moses writes to the Israelites and describes the promised land as a gift, full of cities they did not build, furnished houses they did not buy, wells they didn't dig, as well as vineyards and orchards they didn't plant.[23] And then God in human form turned water into wine, provided Peter with a harvest of fish beyond his wildest dreams, fed five thousand and twelve thousand with a pittance of food, and found the money needed to pay taxes from the belly of a fish.

21. Maxwell, *How Successful People Grow*, 132–33.
22. Ps 105:21 (ESV)
23. Deut 6:10–12 (MSG)

Ultimately, a life of abundance is an invitation to live in the kingdom of God and become like him. In this kingdom, the way of the world ceases to apply to us as we live in accordance with God's promises and provision for us. These promises drive out the fear of the unknown that keeps us from living as if God's promises to us were true and responding in obedience to the promptings of the Spirit. As we increasingly lean into the reality of kingdom abundance, we see that we enter a new way of being that more closely aligns with that of Christ. As Bob Buford writes, "If one advances confidently in the direction of his dreams, and endeavors to live the life which he has imagined, he will meet with a success unexpected in common hours. He will pass an invisible boundary; new, universal, and more liberal laws will begin to establish themselves around and within him; and he will live with the license of a higher order of beings."[24] This higher order of beings was who God created us to be. Not the shadows of ourselves that we settle for in a life of scarcity. Our true self is thus not marked by slavery but by freedom, and this freedom is not a freedom for self but turned outwards to the world. We see that "from God's abundance we get a universe that is too huge and prodigal to be imagined" and "that [this] is a challenge not just to the mind and the imagination, but especially to the heart, to become huge and generous."[25]

We all need to stop living out of the false belief that there is not enough to go around. There is enough and more, if we simply take God at his word. But to accept this truth, we need to believe in our position as the beloved of God. In so doing, we can accept God's abundant provision of relational intimacy and material needs. And as we accept God's infinite blessing, we can go out into our workplaces and the world to multiply the kingdom of abundance by building up and abounding in the love of God to those around us and generously meeting the needs of those without.

---

24. Buford, *Halftime*, 115.
25. Rolheiser, *Sacred Fire*, 279.

AUTHOR'S REFLECTION

As noted in another chapter of this book, I grew up with a low level of affirmation in my life. Another feature of my childhood was growing up solidly middle class. Both of these factors contributed to the development of my own scarcity mindset.

In specific terms, growing up middle class presented a specific irony as it relates to a scarcity mindset. On one hand, I never had to go without basic needs, so I have never experienced that sort of trauma. On the other hand, while growing up middle class means your basic needs are always met, you are then left with feeling the sense of your aspirational wants going unmet. There's always someone better off than you with the things that you want, so of course they must be happier. And without a stable identity rooted in God, it was all to easy to define myself based on what I didn't have, rather than what I did. This of course naturally led to feeling a constant source of material emptiness that I tried to fix by becoming successful enough to buy what I thought I lacked. Clothes, cars, travel, fine dining, watches, etc. I tried it all and none of it worked.

This middle-class background conspired with my lack of affirmation to create a really troubling element of my personality however, and that was a highly insecure tendency to rank and compare people to myself. Without a stable source of identity, I had to build some sort of identity for myself based on superiority to make myself feel good about my own life. I felt good when I was better than other people for whatever reason and felt jealous and angry when I judged that people were doing better than me. While I never expressed how I ranked people in my mind, internally, my thoughts of other people were like a sewer pit that would make a tabloid magazine look positively charitable.

These two elements of my immature mindset led me to evaluate my life based solely on the external metrics of the world. Additionally, if I didn't have what I wanted or felt that I somehow wasn't comparing well enough to my peers, I believed that I needed to change something about my life to achieve the desired outcome

I wanted in life or force myself into a job that would produce the effects that I was looking for.

One of the ways this showed up was how I viewed the city that I lived in. My professional life to date has been entirely in the city of Vancouver, Canada. Vancouver is a beautiful city with a high quality of life, but it has its downsides. For one, if you're a finance professional, there are precious few opportunities to find stimulating and high-paying employment. Those jobs are in Toronto, New York, or any other large global city. The other aspect of Vancouver that's difficult to stomach is the high cost of living. Generally speaking, rents and house prices are not much different than what you'd find in other major cities, but the incomes are much lower.

So when I was young, I did what any rational person would do. I figured I'd just move to where the high-paying finance jobs are, so I could earn the income I thought I deserved and earn the accomplishments I believed would give me a firm sense of identity. Of course, I would move to any of these cities without any consideration to the friendships I had built, the community I had at church, or relationships with my family. Everything (except maybe belief in Jesus) was on the altar of career and material success to make up for my mistaken conclusions about my childhood.

Of course, everything I believed was absolutely meaningless. I was trying to fill a hole that only God could, and fortunately, he prevented me from getting what I wanted and thus saved me from continuing to live a life based on the lies of the false self. Instead of satisfying those shallow desires, I'm deepening in my understanding of God's promises to me, including his commitment to never leave or forsake me. I'm also growing in my belief that my identity is found in what he says about me, rather than what the world says or what I can achieve. I no longer feel like my wants are needs anymore. And I trust that God has a unique path for my life that he will reveal to me in due time that will have its own specific blessings and trials, and that I'm okay with that. Perhaps most important of all, I know that he's with me no matter the circumstances.

DISCUSSION QUESTIONS

1. What are some examples of a scarcity mentality in your life?
2. How do you try to meet your own physical and emotional needs at work?
3. How do you think abundance would free you in your workplace?
4. What's one thing you could do at work to better embrace abundance?

6

Self-Focused to Others-Focused

TYPICALLY, THE BEGINNING PHASE of our lives is an egocentric journey of discovering what our ideal life is based on who God created us to be. This phase of life is meant to be experienced this way, despite our theological acceptance of Jesus' commands to love others as ourselves. Therefore, a primary focus on one's own life at this time is not inherently sinful, but merely reflects the struggle to get our lives together, which is marked by a process of self-discovery, filled with questions such as "Who am I? Where do I find meaning? Who will love me? How do I find love in a world full of infidelity and false promises?"[1] We are predominately focused on how we build the life we desire as we ask questions about ourselves: What do I like? What do I want? How do I get things done? How do I feel? "We have egoistic self-interested desires, and we need those desires in order to accomplish some of the necessary tasks of life: to build an identity, to make a mark on the world, to

---

1. Rolheiser, *Sacred Fire*, 17.

break away from parents, to create and to shine."² And generally speaking, many of us have few, if any, serious responsibilities that would take our attention away from our process of maturation or cause our self-interest to be detrimental to ourselves or others. Simply put, without sufficient focus on the development of our own lives, we run the risk of not finding the life that we were called to, and therefore missing out on the chance of developing a life that is worthwhile to give away. We must first become sufficiently responsible for ourselves as self-sustaining individuals before responsibility is added to us.

If we successfully get our lives together, we look like successful individual contributors, both at work and at home. We are responsible for the tasks assigned to us at work, the errands we need to complete for our personal lives, and for the living expenses that we incur. Crucially, our self-interest can remain primary in this state with few negative consequences. And we can tell we're in this phase by asking ourselves the question, "Where is your ultimate appeal? To self, or to something outside of self?"³ As long as we complete everything at work, keep our life maintained and pay our bills, we are at peace and performing well in our eyes and the opinions of others. Overall, we have yet to be made responsible for anything that is beyond ourselves.

At a certain point, however, this balance will fundamentally change, and we will become responsible not only for ourselves but for the people and responsibilities around us. For some, they are promoted to lead a team, assuming responsibility for the performance and accomplishments of the individuals under their supervision. Others start families and must meet the physical, emotional, spiritual, and intellectual needs of their children. Still others start or begin volunteering for charities or special interest groups, and thus become responsible for meeting the needs of others or coordinating activities for the benefit of others. And there are many additional examples and combinations of examples that we can find ourselves in. The main takeaway remains, however,

---

2. Brooks, *Second Mountain*, 302.
3. Brooks, *Second Mountain*, xvi.

that we not only have to continue meeting our own needs, but we must now shoulder responsibility for others on top of our own interests.

It's at this phase of our careers that a tension emerges. We have grown up with ourselves as *numero uno*, solely responsible for ourselves, and now we must ensure that others get what they need or want as well. Unfortunately, the default approach for many is to retain a self-focused worldview while trying to serve and empower the people that they've been made responsible for. If we continue in this posture, we will become stuck in our development as professionals and people for two reasons.

The first reason is that by remaining self-focused, we become ineffective at meeting our responsibilities and leading other people and run the risk of abusing and objectifying the people around us.

Have you ever had a terrible boss at work? If you haven't had one yet, it's only a matter of time. They tend to have similar qualities. They're obsessed with themselves and how they look to other people, always posturing and positioning themselves to look successful and accomplished. They tend to live out of some combination of striving, capability, and scarcity mindsets. Oftentimes, they are quite successful too; they get a lot done and have great aptitude for accomplishments. But they tend to leave a wreckage in their wake. If you work for them, you can tell they have approximately zero interest in you as a person. All they see in you is a tool for getting stuff done. If you aren't required to help them get something done, you'll never hear from them. They're always too busy to sit down and get to know someone at a personal level, or they'll try to get to know you, but you can tell they don't actually *see* you; getting to know you is just some checkmark on the list of stuff they're supposed to. And no matter how good of a job you do, you never really get much meaningful praise or attention from this type of boss.

This archetypal terrible boss is an all-too-common example of a person that has stayed stuck in a self-focused mindset after receiving responsibility for others. What's concerning is that it's all too easy to end up in that place without knowing it. As mentioned

Self-Focused to Others-Focused

earlier, we all reach a stage in our life where we become responsible for other people, and nowhere is this more evident than at work. We start out as individual contributors, dutifully performing everything that's asked of us, and going above and beyond when required. As thanks for our efforts and conscientiousness, we're often elevated to leadership positions, either coordinating group efforts or becoming responsible for the outcomes of a team.

But when we become responsible for other people, the nature of work changes. It's no longer about our individual actions but how we work *through* other people. Our work becomes less task-oriented and more about empowering other people to do good work through their efforts. When we remain in a self-focused mindset, we often don't make this leap to working through others and instead see people as working *for* us.

When we see people as working for us, they are simply objects for completing whatever needs to be done. We reduce people entirely down to their ability to complete a task that we have been made responsible for. As a result, whenever we are threatened with the risk of a project not going to plan or being late, we "crack the whip" on colleagues and subordinates to ensure we look like we're performing. We also tend to take on all the bad qualities of leadership: controlling, domineering, micro-managing, bullying, etc. If our colleagues exist to get things done in our eyes, then any behavior on our part that accomplishes the desired outcome is justified in our eyes.

Regardless of our consciousness of this mentality, when we work this way, we are guilty of dehumanizing and objectifying those we've been given responsibility for. It's dehumanizing because when we reduce a person's value down to their ability to perform a task, we have removed all the inherent value that person has by being created in the image of God. As we previously discussed the need to see ourselves as the beloved of God apart from our own efforts in the transformation from scarcity to abundance, the same way that Jesus understood his relationship to God, we also need to see the people around us in the same way—possessing inherent worth and value distinct from their ability to produce.

Additionally, when we see people based on what they can do, they essentially become tools to us, completely inanimate objects that further emphasize our objectification of people in the workplace.

Further, if we continue in a self-focused mindset, and the people around us become tools and vehicles for accomplishing *our* dreams, goals, and ambitions, we subject these people to a subtle form of slavery. This is not a slavery of the body, as the people we work with are there of their own volition, but it is a slavery of the heart, as our inward posture sees only the value of what we get out of people, while giving nothing in return. We will pay people and provide them with "opportunities for growth" outwardly, but the interior of our heart will be greedier than Scrooge to our colleagues. As Ronald Rolheiser puts it, "We curse others when we . . . use their lives to build up our own."[4]

Beyond the moral problems of remaining in a self-focused mindset, there are practical consequences too. At a certain point, showing up to the workplace thinking only of ourselves will cease to be effective, and fulfilling our responsibilities will begin to feel like going against the grain. Why is this? Well for one, no one likes being objectified or treated as less than a person! Just think about the example of the terrible boss; very few people want to be around that type of person, regardless of how much they get paid. If we are now tasked with working through people, it becomes infinitely more difficult to be effective if we can't get people to stay around us long enough to complete the task at hand. And if people don't willingly leave on their own, eventually the continual objectification will lead our colleagues to burn out (either physically or emotionally), further impairing our individual and organizational performance.

The second way we become stuck in a self-focused mindset is that we do the right things for the wrong reasons, as we attempt to serve others in an attempt to build our own identity.

So we've discussed how staying self-focused is contrary to our professional development and effectiveness, and we agree that becoming others-focused is the next step. Or perhaps you're naturally

---

4. Rolheiser, *Sacred Fire*, 231.

gifted at being sensitive to the needs of others and serving them, particularly in your vocation. Great! The next step is simply going into the world and making others needs more important than our own, self-sacrificing, and building others up to achieve their goals, right? Obviously giving of ourselves and serving people must be an inherently virtuous practice, right? As Jesus himself said, whoever would be great must be a servant of others.[5]

Not so fast! There is one trap we must address before running headlong into this practice. This trap is the human tendency to seek recognition and acclaim for doing good and selfless works, thereby stealing away the heart of sacrificial love, replacing it with self-centered vanity. It's at this point that we need to move past the outward action and examine the movements of the inner being.

The biggest question we must ask ourselves at this stage is what do I think about as I contemplate or perform an act of service for others? Are we truly giving of ourselves to others out of a deep sense of compassion to help those in need or a desire to bless others? Or are our acts of service in the workplace about cultivating an identity of virtue? In the latter, while we do good works, it's ultimately more about us than it is about the people we serve, thus perpetuating the self-focused mindset we inherit in our immaturity. We might be the manager that gives employees flexibility to care for their families, but our intent is to be known as the progressive or people-centric leader. Or we take on responsibility to lead a charitable committee at work to demonstrate our service to the community or bolster our ESG credentials. We can also twist our Christian faith in the same way, as serving the underprivileged or giving to those in needs is done more as justification of our obedience to the commands of Scripture than it is a desire to earnestly serve another person in love. In each of (although not limited to) these examples, we evidence a greed of the heart where "what we want to accumulate is experience, status, and reputation. More than we want people to recognize us for our money, we want them to recognize us for our good name, our achievements, and

---

5. Mark 10:43 (NIV)

our knowledge. The greed to be known and admired eventually trumps the greed for money."[6]

In short, *why* we do things matters! Even if we progress from living solely for ourselves and begin offering ourselves to satisfy the cries of those around us, if it's done to advance ourselves, we will continue to evidence a self-focused life. There are two warnings from Jesus regarding this way of living:

> "On that day many will say to me, 'Lord, Lord, did we not prophesy in your name, and cast out demons in your name, and do many mighty works in your name?' And then will I declare to them, 'I never knew you; depart from me, you workers of lawlessness.'"[7]

> To some who were confident of their own righteousness and looked down on everyone else, Jesus told this parable: "Two men went up to the temple to pray, one a Pharisee and the other a tax collector. The Pharisee stood by himself and prayed: 'God, I thank you that I am not like other people—robbers, evildoers, adulterers—or even like this tax collector. I fast twice a week and give a tenth of all I get.' But the tax collector stood at a distance. He would not even look up to heaven, but beat his breast and said, 'God, have mercy on me, a sinner.' "I tell you that this man, rather than the other, went home justified before God. For all those who exalt themselves will be humbled, and those who humble themselves will be exalted."[8]

In both of these passages, there is a clear contrast between outer works and the inner posture of the heart. We see people prophesying, casting out demons, and doing mighty works, yet Jesus stating that he doesn't know who they are, or put differently, finding that their heart is not the same as his. We also see a Pharisee dutifully praying, fasting, and giving to the poor, yet finding himself not in right relationship with God. Both evidence good

---

6. Rolheiser, *Sacred Fire*, 90.
7. Matt 7:22–23 (ESV)
8. Luke 18:9–14 (NIV)

works done for the wrong reasons. Deep down, the Pharisee and the miracle performers are out building their own kingdoms, with little regard for those around them, and therefore little regard for God's kingdom. They may look selfless and mature on the outside, but they remain stuck in a self-centered immaturity that is keeping them from advancing into true maturity.

What then? What if we want to move past living for our own lives and serve others with the right intentions? To begin living out a life of service to others with purity of heart, we need to adopt an others-focused mentality. Becoming others-focused is "a process of being formed into the image of Christ for the sake of others."[9] We can start to paint a picture of this process by looking at a management philosophy known as servant leadership. Importantly, we'll look at this philosophy from how the world typically sees it but go deeper to see how it aligns with God's design for human relationships.

Servant leadership, characterized by its originator Robert Greenleaf as the "care taker by the servant-first to make sure that other people's highest priority needs are being served,"[10] is a popular theory. According to Wikipedia, over 270 scholarly articles have been published across 122 academic journals on the subject.[11] While many words have been written about the service-first principles of this management philosophy, having come across the theory several times in more than a decade of a work experience, all too often, it ends up getting pitched based on its ability to improve effectiveness, get more done, and improve outcomes for managers and corporations, all of which reiterate the self-focused view we carry from the early stages of our careers.

But if we're reaching that stage of lives where the conflict of our self-focused approach to work and our responsibilities for other people is producing a pain that has become too uncomfortable in the present, what are we to do? If we are to progress to the next phase of maturity in the workplace, we need to embrace

---

9. Mulholland, *Invitation to a Journey*, 16.
10. Greenleaf Center for Servant Leadership, "What Is Servant Leadership?"
11. Wikipedia, "Servant Leadership."

the *true* biblical principles of servant leadership. How do we adopt an others-focused lens? We start by turning to Paul's letter to the Philippian church, "If you've gotten anything at all out of following Christ, if his love has made any difference in your life, if being in a community of the Spirit means anything to you, if you have a heart, if you care—then do me a favor: Agree with each other, love each other, be deep-spirited friends. Don't push your way to the front; don't sweet-talk your way to the top. *Put yourself aside, and help others get ahead.* Don't be obsessed with getting your own advantage. *Forget yourselves long enough to lend a helping hand.*"[12]

This is a grand vision for our lives. Seeing the people around us with the same importance as ourselves is one of the highest examples of altruism we see in humanity. However, the sheer magnitude of the ambition can feel daunting to those trying to practice it for the first time. If we want to move forward in living out an others-focused life, we need to focus on the steps right in front of us if we want to achiever the bigger goal. With this in mind, here are four more specific examples that can help each of us become more others-focused.

First, to increase the value with which we see other people in our lives, we need to change *how* we see the people around us. This is marked by the transition from "I-It Relationships" to "I-Thou Relationships" that Pete Scazzero describes in *Emotionally Healthy Spirituality*. Drawing on the work of Martin Buber, I-It relationships are characterized by treating people as objects, or simply as a means to an end. In this dehumanization and objectification, we see others as lacking a unique and separate existence from ourselves, causing us to get frustrated with people who don't fit into our plans or agree with us, all as a result of an inward focus. Instead of "I-It" relationships, we are called to cultivate "I-Thou" relationships, recognizing that all of us have been created in God's image and therefore all deserve to be treated with dignity, worth, and respect.[13] Our tendency to see others as less than ourselves is the primary stumbling block to experiencing I-Thou relationships

---

12. Phil 2:1–4 (MSG)
13. Scazzero, *Emotionally Healthy Spirituality*, 172–75.

in our working lives. Therefore, elevating our colleagues to equal positioning with ourselves (or even perhaps taking some down from a pedestal they weren't mean to stand on) is the primary movement that enables us to become more others-focused and in turn, experience a greater depth of relationship in the workplace.

Second, we need to consider how our actions and behaviors impact the people around us. A crucial outcome in transitioning to I-Thou relationships is accepting the unique characteristics and preferences of everyone in our lives. As a result, what is best for us and what we prefer cannot always be what is most edifying to the people we work with. Our colleagues have different learning styles, leadership preferences, working routines, skills, giftings, and personalities than us, among other things. When we force our natural inclinations onto others, we harm and denigrate those around us as we violate their unique character. It's this forceful, undiscerning implementation of what we want that leads so many people to experience us in the most negative light, leaving them with the feeling that we don't value them. Feelings that will far outweigh any accomplishments that they experience at work.

Third, we need to consider the dreams, goals, and ambitions of others. To do this, we can't simply assume that we know what's best for someone else. We need to invest the time to understand what the people around us desire at a soul level. And when we come to this understanding, we need to apply our knowledge of how these individuals become successful in their own way to come alongside them and support them in achieving these goals. It's at this point that we can become real leaders: leaders in spirit rather than in title. Where our leadership is marked by "lifting a person's vision to higher sights, raising of a person's performance to a higher standard, of building a personality beyond its normal limitations."[14] So much of what is wrong with worldly approaches to leadership is the cheap application of surface-level improvements to propel people into cookie cutter goals and a failure to search for everyone's unique vision and equip them to achieve it. It's only when we've truly understood what a person earnestly

---

14. Brooks, *Second Mountain*, 299.

desires and what *they* need to get there that we can begin to apply our own abilities, insights, and efforts to drive them forward. And this is a continual effort, not a one-time transaction. As John Maxwell writes, it's a "daily pouring into others and passing on to them the things that will allow them to run far and achieving beyond what you have done."[15]

Finally, we need to pray for our coworkers. As Christians, we naturally understand the power of prayer, as we invite an infinite God to demonstrate his providence in our lives. But we must not forget how prayer shapes us as we practice it. Prayer has a remarkable ability to change how our minds think; whatever we spend time focusing our attention on during prayer will become something we tend to think about beyond prayer. When we prayerfully consider the people in our lives, what they desire, and how we can bless them, we slowly become people that are continually conscious of the same things when we encounter these people in the flesh.

Embracing these practices and becoming a more selfless person isn't a transformation that is solely for the benefit of the people in our lives, however. What's remarkable about this journey is that we slowly begin to discover that our own best interests are met as we become others-focused. As others flourish in their careers and broader lives, so do we. As John Maxwell observed in a previous chapter, "When you focus more on the wants and needs of others, more of your own wants and needs are met."[16] In a professional sense, when the colleagues on our team are engaged, motivated, and successful, so are we. When the people we lead are gaining recognition for their efforts, we demonstrate our leadership capabilities as a byproduct. We are also the most effective in a practical sense. Not only do we produce our best work in environments led by others-focused individuals, but we end up building up those around us for the long-term. Our coworkers will develop the skills and character traits that will support them for a lifetime when we focus on their development, leaving them with a sense that they are valued as a person. This is a felt experience that will forever

---

15. Maxwell, *How Successful People Grow*, 133.
16. Maxwell, *How Successful People Grow*, 133.

transcend what task or deliverable was needed during that time. In a personal sense, when we cultivate the experience of our colleagues being fully known and seen by us in the workplace, we find that the same intentionality is reflected back to us, satisfying our need to be known and recognized in our workplaces and further developing a sense of workplace community, marked by emotionally gratifying I-Thou relationships.

It's only when we completely reverse our priorities in the workplace and become others-focused that we authentically live out the practice of servant leadership. When our leadership style fully embraces this ethos, the priority of our time at work becomes the best interest of those around us, irrespective of the circumstances and any immediate outcomes. We can thus disentangle how we measure our success from outcomes. Success is now measured by how we invest in the people around us each day. This is crucial if we are to continue living out this way of life, because "if you are sowing only for quick returns in life, then you will usually be unhappy with the outcome ... [but] if you sow continually and abundantly, you can be sure that in due season there will be a harvest."[17] In this paradigm, our sowing is the time and effort we pour into others to help them live their dreams, while the harvest is what we personally receive; two events that will often be separated by a lot of time passing. But when we "consider the success of [our] day based on the seeds [we] sow, not the harvest [we] reap,"[18] as Robert Louis Stevenson put it, we develop the fortitude to continue giving to others each day without knowing what the fruit of that gift will be and develop the patience to eagerly wait for the growth of those around us without regard for the next deadline, quarterly earnings cycle, annual operating plan, or long-term growth forecast.

As we invest in people for the long-term out of our ever-growing sense of focusing on others, we begin to exemplify the only form of leadership that is durable. This type of leadership is durable because it's entirely devoid of force or imposed self-will, the primary mechanisms by which the world, and subsequently

17. Maxwell, *How Successful People Grow*, 136.
18. Maxwell, *How Successful People Grow*, 135.

most organizations and leaders, accomplish their goals. Instead, others-focused leadership is built on the basis of mutual self-giving of individuals as an expression of free will. The enduring nature of this reciprocal dynamic stems from its origin in God as Trinitarian community and subsequently God's intended design for his relationship with humans. Thus, it's only as we begin to live life as God himself experiences it that we can get a taste for a life with eternal significance. As Ronald Rolheiser puts it, "When we act like God, we get to feel like God."[19] Or rather, the care and devotion that we give to those around us that leads to their best interests beyond today simply reflects the nature of human relationships that God intended for us.

With this priority of relationships in mind, we thus see that true leadership is not measured by our accomplishments, either individually or corporately, but by the degree to which we are devoted to each other. As Charles Spurgeon put it, "I would sooner be the leader of six free men, whose enthusiastic love is my only power over them than play the director to a score of enslaved nations. What position is nobler than that of a [leader] who claims no authority and yet is universally esteemed, whose word is given only as tender advice, but is allowed to operate with the force of law? Consulting the wishes of others he finds that they are glad to defer to him. Lovingly firm and graciously gentle, he is the chief of all because he is the servant of all."[20]

AUTHOR'S REFLECTION

The first position I had in my career was as a commercial banker, where I had to seek out new customers, write loan applications, and manage a portfolio of clients. It was a great place to start my career, but after a couple of years, I realized it wasn't where I wanted to spend the rest of my working life. I had been studying for a professional designation and dreamed of working with bigger,

---

19. Rolheiser, *Sacred Fire*, 234.
20. Spurgeon, *Spurgeon's Lectures to His Students*, 187.

more sophisticated businesses, while moving from the suburbs to the downtown core of Vancouver.

My colleagues must have noticed that my heart wasn't in it, so my direct supervisor at the time sat me down and asked me for a full transparency answer about what I wanted to do for a living. The way he asked the question prompted me to respond honestly about what I really wanted. The crucial point here is that my honesty was met with support and warmth by my supervisor, not disapproval and rejection. My supervisor could have fired me on the spot for knowing I didn't want to be there, but instead, he made me a deal. As long as I fulfilled the responsibilities of my current job, he would give me the freedom and flexibility to pursue what I truly desired. Here was a guy who was going to lose a direct report that was helping him manage his own job, but instead of getting defensive and making it about him, chose to help build me up in my own career. As far as I know, he wasn't a Christian either!

To this day, my old boss stands out to me as the type of person I want to be at work: someone who is truly interested and invested in their colleagues to the point of seeking the best interests of those around them instead of for themselves. Someone who is willing to take the time to truly understand who the people around them are and what they dream about. Someone willing to sacrifice short-term performance for the benefit of someone's long-term development. I believe my manager displayed the type of unconditional care that God the Father offers to each of us, and I will always remember him because of that. He was truly others-focused, and to me stands as a perfect real-world example of what it means to live out this belief in the workplace.

DISCUSSION QUESTIONS

1. In what ways are you still self-focused in your career?
2. What are some of the current invitations to serve others in your career?

3. What is your familiarity with servant leadership? How does it change your view of leadership?

4. Which one of the four practices (I-Thou Relationships, Considering our impact on others, Investing time in other's goals, and Prayer) of servant leadership do you feel most compelled to try? Why? After reflection, develop a plan to practice servant leadership at work.

7

Changing the World to Self-Transformation

AT THE TIME OF writing, our world appears to be facing an ever growing laundry list of problems: income inequality, climate change, housing unaffordability, immigration, famine, homelessness, geopolitical instability, gender inequality, excessive debt levels, increasing crime rates, ageing populations, reproductive rights, political polarization, mental health, rising interest rates, addiction, war, global poverty, de-globalization, inflation, corruption, low productivity growth, a decline in democracy, to name a few. Please don't shoot the messenger for omitting any of the issues that you think I missed! Needless to say, there is no shortage of evidence regarding the fallen nature of the world we live in.

Despite the number of issues, one of the remarkable things about human nature is our capacity for agency and the application of individual will. So for many of us, when we see problems in the world, whether large scale issues hitting the headlines or smaller troubles we face day-to-day, we instinctively recognize our ability to improve things through our actions. This shows up in many ways: politics, social movements, and charity work are primary examples. But we also see it in companies trying to address climate change, B Corporations, purpose-driven companies, social enterprises, or firms operating with ESG practices. Examples could also be as simple as helping out friends or a family in need. Christians often express a similar desire for impact as we infuse our faith into efforts to help the world through initiatives like redemptive entrepreneurship, creation care, missional enterprises, or businesses built on biblical principles. In all of these examples and more, we invest ourselves in fixing the problems of the world with good intentions in mind.

We therefore set out with grand ambitions and full of energy to change the world for the better, and we often do. Except once we've fixed one problem, many times others pop up in their stead. This reality is evidenced across decades of time. For example, in 2024, some of the top issues of our time would be the war in Ukraine, a conflict in the Middle East, inflation and housing unaffordability, carbon emissions and climate change, and rising crime and homelessness in major cities. Go back roughly fifty years to the 1970s, and what were some of the primary issues of the day? The Vietnam War, the Cold War, inflation led by an oil supply crisis, concerns about environmental catastrophe, as well as rising crime rates and concerns about urban decay. Sound familiar? It's as if nothing has changed in over half a century.

Alternatively, when we go out seeking to solve problems, what we once thought were technical or structural issues that could be solved with truth, ingenuity, and elbow grease turn out to be the result of people. When this happens, the desire to improve then becomes a mission to change people or remove them: eliminate all corrupt politicians and businesspeople, get all the criminals in jail, or fire a difficult coworker. Or if we can't make any of those results happen, we carry around that desire in our hearts, shading all our thoughts, feelings, and actions with the intent to remove people from situations as the desired outcome.

Seeing people as the root of all problems in the world is in one sense accurate but in another sense misguided. For one, it's entirely unreasonable to think that people will simply change themselves to align with our expectations. Further, when we see individual people as barriers to progress that simply need to be eradicated to arrive at the solution, we fall into the sort of dehumanization that has been at the root of so many episodes of humanity's ugly past. This way of trying to "fix" the world always believes that the ends justify the means. Ironically, the spirit of injustice that many of us arrive at can lead us to think that the destruction of other people groups or individuals is what would solve the problem today, when it would only perpetuate the cycle. We are appalled at the physical acts of historical dehumanization but seem to have no issue dehumanizing people today with our words or thoughts.

However, what is most pernicious about our desire to solve problems, regardless of the means by which we accomplish them, is when we make our satisfaction with life dependent on the resolution of said problems. Or to put it differently, believing that we will only experience joy when we've changed the world. As John Mark Comer says, "If life is about problem solving to make ourselves happy, it becomes a game of whack-a-mole."[1] It seems that no matter how many problems we, or the collective human population, solve, it never seems to satisfy us on the inside. Whether the party we voted for wins, we get a new boss that we get along with, we reduce the number of young people with depression, or invent a product that reduces toxic emissions, we always end up feeling the same way after the fact.

Our dissatisfaction with any measurable improvement (or lack thereof) stems from three reasons. The first of these reasons is the unchecked sense of pride that we carry into our view of the world. This pride shows up in our overestimation of our ability to rightly judge the root cause of the problems we see in the world, stemming from an emotionally unhealthy desire to feel superior to the people around us. As Karl Barth writes, "The root and origin of sin is the arrogance in which man wants to be his own and his neighbor's judge."[2] We often also enter into a position of judgment blind to our own vulnerability and contribution to the problems of

---

1. Comer, *Active and Passive Spirituality*, May 19, 2019.
2. Barth, *Church Dogmatics*, 231–34.

the world, further evidencing why so often our diagnosis of injustice is faulty. As Jesus said, "First take the log out of your own eye, and then you will see clearly to take the speck out of your brother's eye."[3] How often do we fail to see the log in our own eyes as we believe we correctly assess the speck in the eyes of those around us and in the broader world?

The second source of our dissatisfaction arises from the overestimation of our capacity to fix the problems we identify in the world. Even if we could truly identify the complicated and multivariate nature of each issue we encounter, we would still run into the limits of our individual agency and ability to affect change. As Thomas Kelly writes, "We cannot die on every cross, nor are we expected to."[4] For many reading this, you will push back at the ideas of any sense of limits regarding your ability to positively impact the world. Historical examples of people that advanced justice or solved problems will be top of mind, particularly given our tendency to isolate large events and attribute them to individual actors. But have you ever asked yourself who gave you the responsibility to fix whatever issue you've become invested in? As David Brooks says, "You should ignore 99% of these moments of obligation, no matter how guilty it makes you feel. The world is full of problems, but very few are the problems you are meant to address."[5] Or have you considered how you have come to see yourself as the primary factor in whether something in the world changes or not? As difficult as it is to admit, regardless of the size of an issue or degree of evil, "the world will not fall apart if we cease our activities" because "life on this side of heaven is an unfinished symphony. We accomplish one goal and then immediately are confronted with new opportunities and challenges . . . [where] ultimately we will die with countless unfinished projects and goals."[6] Underneath our overestimation of individual ability is at heart an overestimation of our own significance. We *want* to be significant because we believe

---

3. Matt 7:5 (ESV)
4. Kelly, *Testament of Devotion*, 64–65.
5. Brooks, *Second Mountain*, 120.
6. Scazzero, *Emotionally Healthy Spirituality*, 155.

that by doing so, we can find a sense of importance, even if that sense of importance is unconnected to the true solution of the cause we feel compelled to fix. As Jamie Winship describes Moses' early life in Egypt, "[He] really did make a mistake by moving to help his people without first asking God for wisdom."[7] But as we try to manufacture that sense of importance by becoming involved in the world's problems, we lose sight of the fact that "God is at work taking care of the universe [and that] He manages quite well without us having to run things."[8]

The question of *why* we want to feel significant leads us to our third and most fundamental source of dissatisfaction with changing the world. That is, the mistaken belief that our efforts to change the world are the primary avenue by which we achieve a sense of significance in our lives. And this achievement of a sense of significance comes from the message, either from the church, culture, parents, peers, or otherwise, that our individual worth is based on what we can do for the world. Because of this, our "eternal value [is] rooted in what [we can] accomplish,"[9] and we subsequently live from a sense of "missionalism," which is "the belief that the worth of one's life is determined by the achievement of a grand objective."[10] What is remarkable about this way of living is how it cuts across both "virtuous" efforts to change the world and "baser" forms of ambition. Whether our desire to change the world is through an enterprise that advocates for social justice or is an innovative new start-up that is worth billions of dollars, both evidence a heart posture of seeking validation through one's efforts. Beyond the nature of the organizations themselves, it's also amazing to see how missionalism pervades secular *and* Christian culture; believers and non-believers alike are running around the world trying to drum up a sense of worthiness by doing the "right things" with their lives. In fact, if anything, the strength of the sense of missionalism is amplified in the lives of Christians because of

---

7. Winship, *Living Fearless*, 104.
8. Scazzero, *Emotionally Healthy Spirituality*, 155.
9. Jethani, *With*, 90.
10. Jethani, *With*, 89.

a mistaken understanding that their eternal destiny depends on what they do for God in the world and "that what mattered was not God's love for them, but how much they could accomplish for him."[11] But what unites all of these examples—spiritual to secular, social causes to successful commercial enterprises—is the question of every insecure human heart: "How can I prove that I am valuable."[12] And it is the conflict of groping for a sense of value through the temporal efforts of our own hands that ultimately leaves us restless and dissatisfied, regardless of what vocation or social cause we choose to devote our time to. At a certain point, we realize, that no matter what we do, no amount of effort or perceived sense of progress will answer the question of whether we're personally valuable or not.

So where does that leave us on an individual level? If it's difficult for us to correctly identify problems in the world, let alone fix them through our individual capacity, or find evidence of our inherent worth, what are we to do? First and foremost, we need to put God back in his rightful place as sovereign Lord of *all* creation, thereby recognizing his work in the world, despite any evidence to the contrary. As Paul writes, "We know that in all things God works for the good of those who love him."[13] For many of us, we have become so action-oriented that we have lost sight of the fact that God is not calling us into service every time something goes wrong in the world; he alone is working all things for our good, both the good and the bad. In fact, when we look at Genesis, we see that God's prohibition to Adam and Eve was to eat of the tree of the *knowledge of good and evil*.[14] With this in mind, it appears that God's original design for human flourishing didn't include involving us in cases of moral judgment. It seems that God knew our limited perspective as humans would always fall short of God's perfect justice and subsequently didn't intend on giving us this responsibility. Just think about how much historical damage has

11. Jethani, *With*, 82.
12. Jethani, *With*, 88.
13. Rom 8:28 (ESV)
14. Gen 2:9 (NIV)

been done by humans out of a reactionary sense of injustice: the military aggression of Germany that led to World War II was largely a reaction to the punitive measures France sought from Germany as revenge for World War I; much of the Rwandan genocide stems from a circle of violence in response to the past injustices of ruling Tutsi and Hutu governments; the French Revolution began as a rebellion against an indulgent and indifferent aristocracy but ended up murdering opposing and moderate voices in pursuit of political expediency. It only takes a small list of examples to see the apparent wisdom of God's intention.

As we come to know that solving the world's problems is not our primary responsibility, we can in turn accept the reality that the root of evil in the world is the condition of the selfish human heart. With this truth in mind, we can thus see that nothing we do to fix the world through external changes will result in enduring change unless people themselves change on the inside. Therefore, no amount of policy, technology, economic incentive or physical relief will in and of itself change the nature of humanity's heart, and we can therefore accept the limitations of our efforts to change the world while freeing ourselves from the self-destructive pressure we have placed on ourselves to justify our life through good deeds. Further, when see that the collective experience of humanity is the natural result of a world full of imperfect hearts wandering aimlessly and alone in search of their own view of the promised land, and that of our own accord, we cannot guide enough people back to restore the world as a whole, we can find peace as "we realize that the deepest problems cannot be solved, but only embraced, forgiven, released, and accepted as an act of trust [in God]."[15]

But surely there is a role for us all to play in the renewal of the world? Surely God isn't calling us to indifference towards the problems we see? Surely the feeling inside me that tells me something is wrong in the world is meaningful? Surely there is something we can all do to make the kingdom of heaven more present today? The answer to all of these questions is a resounding yes. Indeed, the answer to these questions begins with ourselves, when we start with

---

15. Comer, *Active and Passive Spirituality*, May 19, 2019.

seeing the problems of the world originating in our own hearts and thus begin the journey of self-transformation.

What is self-transformation? First and foremost, it's the recognition that the problems of this world originate in each individual heart and therefore that the transformation of ourselves as individuals into the perfect image of Christ is the surest route to creating lasting impact in the world around us. As Aleksandr Solzhenitsyn wrote, "The line separating good and evil passes not through states, nor between classes, nor between political parties either—but right through every human heart—and through all human hearts."[16] Put more simply, we realize that the problem is actually inside of us, instead of the outside world. David Brooks echoes this when he writes that "I no longer believe that we can change anything in the world until we have first changed ourselves."[17] This way of looking at the problems of the world reflects the humility that many of us so desperately need, as changing who we are, and who we become, is the thing we have the most direct agency over, particularly when compared with our desire to change the world generally or other people more specifically. Of course, we are not entirely responsible for our transformation; God is the author and perfecter of our faith and thus our guide in the journey into Christlikeness, working in our lives as we actively pursue him and passively allow him to work in our lives through what we can't control. But the fact remains, even with God's role in this journey, our own responsibility in choosing and becoming like Christ is the one thing we have the most influence over in this world. We can't fix the world's problems, but we *can* change who we are.

So if we can change who we are, and that is the surest route to bringing God's kingdom to earth, what does that look like practically? And more specifically, what does that mean for my career? There are a number of useful ways to think about affecting change in our own lives. In his book *Practicing the Way*, John Mark Comer summarizes his working theory of change as marked by: 1) teaching, where our ideas about God, the world, and ourselves

---

16. Solzhenitsyn, *Gulag Archipelago*, 312.
17. Brooks, *Second Mountain*, 79.

are reformed according to biblical truth, 2) practices in which we begin to live the way we want to live in light of teaching, 3) community that supports our attempts to practice a new way of life and reinforces our beliefs, 4) the Holy Spirit and his active leading and direction of our lives in accordance with Gods' will, 5) suffering and the ability of difficulty and trials to shape who we are, and 6) time and the compounding impact of all five influences shaping us.[18] Dallas Willard described the pattern that leads to self-transformation as marked by Vision, Intention and Means, where we gain a new belief for who we want to become and how we live, change our intentions such that we desire to live as we now believe, and then identify and practice the means by which we become who we want to be.[19] One final construct that we can understand the practical realities of self-transformation is a process where we put on a new self that is driven by the knowledge of ourselves as the image of God.[20] As we replace our worldly beliefs about work with who God wants us to be as Christ and therefore how we show up at work, we thus are led in to confession and repentance, where we acknowledge the gap between who God calls us to be and where we currently are. Finally, we put on the new self[21] and begin intentionally living our lives in accordance with the new belief about what God says about us and our work.

What then is the new belief, vision, or teaching that we need to start the process of self-transformation with? Our new belief is twofold: 1) we must come to understand that our significance is not based on what we are able to do for God but from his affection towards us that pre-exists our being and 2) replace our attempts to change the world with the hope of bringing the kingdom of heaven into the present with an ambition to experience the quality of life that marks the kingdom of heaven in our individual lives.

Our repentance is thus realizing that our attempts to change the world have got this process backwards. God's design is not that

---

18. Comer, *Practicing the Way*, 101–14.
19. Willard, *Renovation of the Heart*, 85–90.
20. Col 3:10 (ESV)
21. Eph 4:22–24 (NIV)

changes to the external world will produce internal change in our hearts but rather that self-transformation is the vehicle by which God uses us to change the world in alignment with his kingdom, reflecting Jesus' parable of the mustard seed, where what is small and invisible ends up becoming a large tree that birds nest in.[22]

The action then becomes making intentional choices to experience the kingdom of heaven in our individual lives. This kingdom is marked by the fruits of the spirit: "Love, joy, peace, forbearance, kindness, goodness, faithfulness, gentleness and self-control."[23] Regardless of the context we find ourselves in and the work we do, we can all intentionally grow in our practice and experience of these fruits. We can realize that "God can use virtually any setting to do his deeper work in us in order to help us reach a state of imperturbable calm."[24] As a result, we can bring God's kingdom to earth, and especially to our workplaces, when we become the kind of people that live as if the world has already been renewed and God's kingdom is already here (which it is!). Just take a minute and reflect on how different our workplace experiences would be if everyone bore a little more of the fruits of the spirit every day.

However, self-transformation is not an ambition that solely focuses on our individual lives. It is rather the proper sequence of events that produces outward change. As Robert Mulholland writes, our self-transformation is "a process of being formed into the image of Christ for the sake of others."[25]

First and foremost, a commitment to transform into the image of Christ and experience the fruits of the spirit allows us to see the world clearly—because the world is full of complex problems produced by broken and imperfect people—yet not rushing towards others in judgment and creating us/them dynamics or proposing simple solutions that ignore the nuance that characterizes so much of our human condition. Our view of people also changes: we can see politicians, business leaders, friends, coworkers, and celebrities

22. Matt 13:31–32 (NIV)
23. Gal 5:22–23 (NIV)
24. Sittser, *Water from a Deep Well*, 90.
25. Mulholland, *Invitation to a Journey*, 16.

Changing the World to Self-Transformation

for who they are, not as solely responsible for the problems we face. Further, as our faith in God and patience for his restoration grows, we find more peace with the present, like Brother Lawrence, who, when contemplating the "miseries and sins he heard of daily in the world ... was so far from wondering at them, that, on the contrary ... was surprised that there were not more, considering the malice sinners were capable of; that for his part he prayed for them; but knowing that God could remedy the mischiefs they did when He pleased, he gave himself no farther trouble."[26]

Our commitment to self-transformation and the resulting freedom from the belief that our significance is based on what we do also enables us to break the cycle of vulnerability in the world that stems from people working out of that idol. Recall the concept of missionalism mentioned earlier in this chapter. Our world is filled with people trying to conjure up a sense of self-worth by changing the world but are in turn becoming hammers that see a world entirely filled with nails, smashing everything because the ends justify the means, and producing a cohort of followers and enemies in their wake. As Skye Jethani writes, "If a [leader's] sense of worth is linked to the impact of his or her [career], guess what [people] under that [leader's] care are told is the most important? And so a new generation of people who believe their value is linked to their accomplishments is birthed."[27] And this next generation, "marching onward in life ... become big people and move on with their malfunctioning souls into workplace, profession, citizenship, and leadership. From them proceeds the next generation of wounded souls. Many of these now 'big people,' and perhaps 'the best and brightest' try hard to rectify the situation. They sponsor sickeningly shallow solutions to the human problem, such as 'education,' 'diversity,' or 'tolerance.'"[28] The cycle, unfortunately, continues abreast today. However, when our souls become free from the pressure to change the world and discover our identity as children of God, we are able to break this cycle, as we cease to pass on this

---

26. Lawrence, *Practice of the Presence of God*, 6.
27. Jethani, *With*, 92.
28. Willard, *Renovation of the Heart*, 192.

unhealthy dynamic to those around us. Breaking this cycle starts with rediscovering our own worth that's entirely unconnected to what we can do but completely determined by what God says about us. It's this truth that is what we're searching for when we mistakenly try to prove our own importance by changing the world. And it's this same truth that produces the joy that "filled Paul . . . in prison while not accomplishing anything tangibly for God."[29]

Finally, our commitment to self-transformation allows us to see ourselves as we truly are and therefore what our unique calling in the kingdom of heaven is. Self-transformation frees us from being driven by reactivity to external events or compulsion to prove or justify ourselves. Rather, it positions us to see the specific part of our world that we are uniquely equipped to co-labor with God in, out of joy and willful service to others. As John Mark Comer writes, "Jesus will lay one small part of his universal heart of love [on each of us]. We will find our hearts drawn to particular justice issues, people groups, neighbor families, or lines of work. And it will feel like joy."[30]

Amidst the value of self-transformation to ourselves and others, it is also the only route towards lasting and enduring change. The eternal nature of this change stems from the absence of any force or coercion. Change without any externally imposed will reflects God's desires for us; he does not call anyone into relationship with him who does not want it—neither does he force us to change without our assent. Additionally, so much of human "progress" is at root based on the imposition of force. A great deal of our society is built on getting people to do what they don't naturally want to do out of fear of repercussions. For better or worse, this reflects a wise acceptance of the fallenness of human nature and the need for rules to minimize bad behavior and effectively create an orderly society. But when the same mentality is applied to improve civilization or produce moral behavior, the ineffectiveness of force to produce good is apparent. As Dallas Willard writes, "The effort to change our behavior without inner transformation is precisely what we

---

29. Jethani, *With*, 92.
30. Comer, *Practicing the Way*, 151.

see in the current shallowness of Western [Civilization] that is so widely lamented and in the notorious failures of [leaders]."[31]

It is this juxtaposition of the shallow application of force to produce morality and the continual failure of all people to be moral that lays bare the truth that our efforts to change the world, through our own efforts and particularly through the use of force, are not capable of producing the results that we want. Because "it is who we are in our thoughts, feelings, dispositions, and choices—in the inner life—that counts [and therefore] profound transformation is the only thing that can definitively conquer outward evil."[32] In other words, "The only reliable force of change would come from something much more powerful than human strength: true metanoia, the conversion of mind and heart."[33] So if we do not prioritize our inner lives in our pursuit of self-transformation into the image of Christ, we do not stand any chance removing evil from our world and seeing a greater physical manifestation of the kingdom of heaven, regardless of how much we invest our own efforts in doing so.

However, when we instead pursue self-transformation, experience the fruits of the spirit in our own lives, and become people who live lives of love, joy, and peace, we create a model of living that inspires other people to want the same for themselves. When the fruit of our lives invites other people to become like Christ, through acts of free will, we are thus participating in the process of eternal change that we are seeking in our desire to change the world but without resorting to the blunt tactics of humanity that cannot produce it. Instead of correcting the people around us, we create a connection with them that leads to change. Or in David Brooks' words, "Relationship is the driver of change."[34] And so as we experience self-transformation, leading those around us to desire and pursue self-transformation for themselves, and multiplying outward from that, our small, individual effort ends up having

31. Willard, *Renovation of the Heart*, 79.
32. Willard, *Renovation of the Heart*, 24.
33. Adubato, "Metaphysical Promise of the Consumer Society."
34. Brooks, *Second Mountain*, 72.

a far more magnified effect through the work of the Holy Spirit. It turns out that a dedicated ambition to become our best selves in Christ ends up producing the largest and most lasting impact. As John Maxwell writes, "If we focus on personal character, we make the world a better place. If we do that our entire lives, we've done the best thing we can do to improve our world."[35] And when we focus on personal character and our transformation by God's love for us, we are then motivated to go out into the world and serve others in accordance with God's good will, instead of our own.

While we will never reach heaven on this side of earth, as we move from a feeble attempt to change the world to embracing self-transformation as a primary ambition, we can experience a taste of it as the fruits of the spirit—love, joy, peace, forbearance, kindness, goodness, faithfulness, gentleness, and self-control—increasingly characterize the lives that we live. And, as we experience the freedom that comes from rediscovering the importance of self-transformation, we can find rest for our ambitious selves, knowing that in partnership with God, we've done all that we have been personally called to do with our time on this earth and for eternity.

AUTHOR'S REFLECTION

Living out of a "changing the world" mentality influenced the way I saw the world in a variety of ways. From a superficial perspective, I was very emotionally invested in politics and related debates, to the point that much of how I felt during a day depended on what the current government (or governments in other countries) was doing and whether it aligned with my own beliefs and values. I always dreamed of some sort of "promised land" where everyone would see things the way I did, and then society could truly flourish. I was also a big believer in the value of apologetics. I naively thought that if people would just hear the truth, their hearts would change, and many would come to Christ.

---

35. Maxwell, *How Successful People Grow*, 82–83.

My changing-the-world mentality also impacted how I viewed my career. I couldn't just simply have a career that I enjoyed and met my needs, I needed some combination of impact and influence. I always imagined that I would use my success in the workplace to change something systematically (say employment ownership or climate change) that would bring about more of God's kingdom and make me look good in the process.

The problem was that I didn't embody much of Christ's qualities. I was stubborn, argumentative, completely disconnected from my emotions, leery of helping strangers, and unwilling to embrace the messiness of people or relationships. Needless to say, my personal qualities were entirely incompatible with the vision I had for myself. Sure, I did the "right" things by serving at my church, leading small groups, and volunteering for humanitarian causes. But none of these activities ever felt joyful. It was more like a dutiful slog to somehow prove that I did what the Bible said, rather than my actions being a natural outpouring of love.

There has been no one event or transcendent experience that has led me out of my past way of changing-the-world thinking. It's been the accumulation of time, many small, seemingly insignificant influences, and God's providence in my life. But I believe it does revolve around one idea, and that's God's infinite goodness towards us. As I've mentioned elsewhere, each human heart either consciously or unconsciously is asking the question "am I valuable?" And if we're not going to God with that question, we're going to look to something other than him to answer that question. And I sure was guilty of not going to God with that question.

Fortunately, at a certain point, God showed me that he didn't need me to do anything for him and that I was valuable to him irrespective of what I did for him. This despite constant messages from childhood that I was what I could produce or do. So many of us believe with their minds what God says about us as his children, but far too many have not let that truth penetrate their hearts. But as that truth began to enter the deepest depths of my soul, I began to see that what God really wanted for me was to become more like

Christ and that I wasn't responsible for the end goal. All I had to do was say yes to each small step along the way.

Now, as my performative expectations of myself begin to fade into the background, I feel far less pressure to build a life of significance for myself or to see people as obstacles that need to be put into place to validate my own judgment of how the world has fallen short of God's kingdom. I no longer need to look at my career as a source of eternal identity. I believe that God is actually in control of everything, even when all evidence is to the contrary in my eyes. For once, I have at least a modicum of patience and understanding for people who are different from me or don't see things the way that I do. In no small way, peace has come to pervade my life in a way that I would only have dreamed of if I had accomplished all that I wanted to do.

DISCUSSION QUESTIONS

1. Are there any problems in the world that keep you from experiencing peace? If yes, reflect on why this problem(s) gets in the way of experiencing peace today.

2. Is your life marked by "missionalism" (where we believe our eternal value is rooted in what we can accomplish)? Why or why not?

3. Do you agree that the biggest ambition in our working lives is to experience the fruits of the Spirit? Why or why not?

4. Which fruit of the Spirit (love, joy, peace, forbearance, kindness, goodness, faithfulness, gentleness, and self-control) do you feel called to practice at work? Why?

8

Control to Surrender

IF I WAS ASKED what I thought the dominant idol of our modern Western secular culture is, based on my experience of having lived in it my entire life, I would say control. The default assumption of most people in this culture, and especially in the workplace, is that we are in control. We're in control of our routines, our careers, our goals, our dreams, our time, our money, our jobs, the businesses that we run, the people we lead, our plans, our futures, our kids, etc. We also tend to think that we're in control of many of the problems we face too. Climate change, political division, mental health, crime, homelessness, income inequality, illness, and health all have solutions according to the idol of control.

Partly, this reflects how effective we have been at controlling segments of the world. Just take a look at the number of inventions that have occurred over the past three hundred years and what they're able to do: steam engines, sewing machines, hydraulics, anesthetics, internal combustion engines, canning, wristwatches, telegraphs, electromagnets, gas stoves, lawn mowers, Morse code, fertilizers, cement, safety pins, flush toilets, batteries, dynamite, stainless steel, the light bulb, radio, automobiles, wind turbines, zippers, electric ovens, airplanes, gas turbines, television, penicillin, nylon, nuclear fission, rockets, radiocarbon dating, video games, hard disk drives, lasers, personal computers, high-speed rail, microprocessors, GPS, CD-ROM, DNA profiling, the Internet, Bluetooth, DVD, online dating, MP3 players, the smartphone, e-readers, cancer therapies, cryptocurrencies, genome editing, RNA vaccines, and generative AI.

We have become so good at controlling *some* parts of the world that our assumption is that we're in control of *all* parts of the world. Want further proof that our cultural belief is that we're in control of everything? Just observe what happens collectively or individually when we experience things that are out of our control. A great example is the recent COVID pandemic. How many opinion pieces were written that made a point something along the lines of suggesting that it was somehow preventable or asked questions wondering how it could have happened in the first place. Or look at how people tend to react to things that happen in their own lives: job loss, death of a loved one, misbehaving kids, or just plain old unmet expectations.

Regardless of the individual example discussed, the extremity of our reactions to things that happen to us that are beyond our control illustrates our cultural bias to the idol that we're in the driver's seat of life. And beyond our reactions to various experiences, our tendency to propose solutions to whatever we're facing also emphasizes this default assumption. Whenever we encounter the unexpected, our first impulse is to take control of the situation. If it's political, we want to tax more or spend more; if it's relational, we want to cut people out of our lives or manage other people's behavior; if it's environmental, we want to restrict polluting activities; or if it's financial, we want to save more or invest in products with risk-free returns.

And nowhere does our modern human tendency towards control show up more prevalently than in the workplace. Our mindset towards career and work is rife with the underlying message that we are individually in control of our destinies. Whether it's career advice, inspirational (or promotional) LinkedIn posts, self-help books, leadership training, life coaches, formal education, professional development programs, or what have you, they all tend to operate on the assumption that we are in control of what we want. As a result, if we believe that we're in control, all we need to do is add the right ingredients to our life, apply effort, and like a mystical potion master, we watch the life of our dreams jump out of the cauldron. Or maybe it's more like when the photo you took combines with the right filter to make your post go viral. Whatever metaphor makes the most sense to you, you get the idea.

It should be no surprise that we believe this is true because our culture is awash with messages that promote the idea that we're in control, particularly when it comes to our careers. From the multi-billionaire founder of a successful start-up, to the athlete who overcame the odds to make it professionally, to the immigrant who broke through barriers to create a new life in a foreign land and provide for their family. We all love a good story that reminds us that hard work pays off and confirms to us that if we just set our minds to something, we can do anything we want to. And these messages have their place. They can encourage us when we're filled with disappointment and on the verge of giving up or give us that little boost we need to get a project over the finish line. And during the immature phase of our lives, these messages are powerful and entirely positive. When we're studying in high school to get good grades for university, sustained effort is the clearest route to performing well in class. Or when we're searching for our first career job after university, the biggest risk for a young person is giving up too soon. But these messages do have a dark side: they implicitly tell us that we can do anything in this world, and the only thing stopping us from achieving our dreams is effort.

This mindset of control is also reflected in how we see success stories of other people, where what we're reading for is tips on how to control our lives so we can also get what we want. The way that the media tends to tell these success stories only exacerbates this point (and because it sells subscriptions or magazines, not because it's designed to help you). The key to all of these stories comes down to two things: 1) highlighting a successful person's "big break," and 2) making the reader feel like they can achieve similar success if they follow a similar path as the subject. The problem with the latter point is that success is not as simple as following a simple path that we're in control of. If all we needed to do to become billionaires was follow Jeff Bezos's path, well, there'd be a lot more billionaires in the world (or the billionaires wouldn't be billionaires). The reality is that all of the external factors that allow specific people to be successful do not remain constant for the next person trying to replicate the first person's success. The passage of time always creates change and is a constant force that's reshuffling the deck for everyone. Additionally, when these stories focus on a 'big break,' they make success appear as if getting to the next level is a matter of simply pursing our dreams long enough until some magical moment finally appears out of nowhere as a reward for hard work, causing the rest of us to stay in the same spot, chasing the same miracle, hoping in vain that one day it'll all be different.

Malcolm Gladwell spoke about this at length in his book *Outliers*. He rigorously studied numerous examples of highly successful people to try and understand what led to that success. For example, he identified Bill Gates as someone highly successful. But Bill Gates was born to a family that was well off enough to send him to a private school that had a computer he could learn to program on, when computers were rare and extremely expensive.[1] Not only that, he was born at a time when the computer industry was still nascent, creating a window for many individuals with programming skills to develop software for a burgeoning market. Gladwell even surmises that if Bill Gates had been born two years earlier or two years later, he would've been too old or too young to capitalize on the opportunities in the software industry.[2] In other words, we can do everything the same as Bill Gates, but we'll never get the same result as he did. And this is true for every other externally successful person you can identify. Some of the lessons from another person's life may not even apply to us, further confusing the sense that we're in control of our careers. As Gladwell

---

1. Gladwell, *Outliers*, 43.
2. Gladwell, *Outliers*, 65.

summarizes his analysis and its implications, "We pretend that success is exclusively a matter of individual merit . . . but success was not just of [one's] own making. It was the product of the world in which [one] grew up."³

So, if control is our default assumption for how we look at our careers and the related expectations we have of them, how did we get to this place to begin with? I doubt any of us popped out of the womb thinking that we're in control of the world, yet here we are. There are two answers to this question.

The first reason for why we end up thinking we're in control is because we are in fact in control of *some* things (both individually and societally, as noted previously). As we've discussed at length in previous chapters, there's an interesting dynamic at play where how we experience life as immature adults ceases to be a useful guide as we age. As it relates to control, what we find is that we do exercise control over ourselves as we navigate becoming the people we want to grow up to be. The difference between whether we pass an exam or complete university is based on whether we study or not. Similarly, whether we retain gainful employment or not is based on our commitment to show up to work. We only discover what we like if we decide to invest our time and take some risks as we try new things. And we only find out what we're good at if we stay consistent enough to turn an interest into a profession. At the center of all these transitions is us; our choice to do something is the primary vector by which our lives change, and whether we get what we want, or not. The problem begins when we assume that because we're in control of *some* things in our lives, we are therefore in control of *everything*.

The other reason why we come to believe that we're in control of our careers is a result of how modern thought has evolved through time, especially as it relates to history and our interpretation of historical events. To illustrate this, we can turn to the second epilogue of Leo Tolstoy's *War and Peace*,⁴ where he provides

---

3. Gladwell, *Outliers*, 67.
4. Tolstoy, *War and Peace*, 1267–1306.

a critical analysis of the study of history. My summary of Tolstoy's analysis is as follows:

History began with "ancient" thinking, whereby the analysis and interpretation of historic events was primarily through the expression of the will of deities or a deity. Thus, everything that was encountered in daily life or in history was reconciled through the intention of God or gods. In place of ancient thinking came the field of modern historical analysis, where the outcomes of history were attributed to the power of great people and their expression of that power. The conclusion that history came down to the whims of individually powerful people, while generally accepted, also existed at the same time as humans understood from experience that they were at least in control of some things in their lives.

However, the mode of thinking whereby history is determined centrally by the actions of a specific group of people has gone on to become the lens by which we interpret the events of our own lives, and subsequently, how we think about the future. Put differently, as modern people, we've come to conflate a historian's interpretation of the past with how we express our free will in daily life, leading us to believe that we are in control of our entire destiny.

This is of course not true. It's not true because historical analysis actually errs in its reduction of historical events to the decisions and actions of powerful people. As Tolstoy shrewdly observes, history is the result of free will, and what he refers to as inevitability. In his thinking, inevitability is the idea that only a specific number of things can happen in a moment, and those are governed by external factors. The external factors that Tolstoy identified as governing all people (and therefore us) are 1) our relation to the external world, 2) our relation to time, and 3) our relation to the causes leading to the moment or action that we decide.

Therefore, true freedom, the idea that we're entirely in control of our lives, is a mirage. True freedom requires us to be outside of time, absent of external forces of causation, and fully knowledgeable of the entire chain of causation leading up to the moment we find ourselves in, all of which are impossible for humans.

To reiterate, we have come to believe that we're in control of our lives because our experiences in early adulthood reinforce the concept that we are in control of some things, while our cultural narrative has borrowed a historian's lens of seeing history through the actions of so-called great people and applied it to our own lives, making each of us as the central character writing our own story. When this is the framework that we approach our professional lives with, we thus regard our careers or our callings as things that are in our control and entirely up to us to coordinate as we see fit.

However, nothing could be further from the truth. For us to be in control of our callings, we would need to be entirely free. Free from time, causation, and prior events. For us to be truly free, and therefore truly in control, we would have to be something other than human. We would have to be God, as God is the only being that is truly free from the constraints that we face as humans. Therefore, if it's true that we are not completely free, we are thus not the authors of our callings and stories. And if God is the only true free being, he must be the only one capable of being the author of our calling. As Eugene Peterson writes, "If we are going to live appropriately, we must be aware that we are living in the middle of a story that was begun and will be concluded by another. And this other is God."[5] It's the acknowledgement of God's authorship of both the human story and our own that is required for us to see the fulfillment of our calling and that "our stories are given meaning not because they are our stories but because they are located within the story of salvation history."[6] It's only when we surrender to his invitations and leadings that we can find the significance that we desire from our vocations. We need to realize that "God is the mover and [we] are the one moved upon."[7] So often, our professional experience is a letdown because we've settled for a small life written on our own terms, instead of allowing ourselves to get caught up in a greater story that God has been writing before us and will continue after us. We would prefer to isolate ourselves

---

5. Peterson, *Run with the Horses*, 37.
6. Sittser, *Water from a Deep Well*, 217.
7. Brooks, *Second Mountain*, 237.

into a small pocket of the world that we feel we can control instead of entering an interplay between us and a larger world that we can't control with God as our guide.

To step into this grander story with God as the author and guide requires one thing, however. It requires us to live a life of surrender to him. We must learn to distinguish "the difference between being called and being driven."[8] We must exchange our lives based on the illusion of control for lives based on total surrender to God and his greater work in humanity and the universe. As John the Baptist said, "He must increase, but I must decrease."[9]

We see a life of surrender to God perfectly exampled in the life of Jesus. Think about all of the external developments that preceded Jesus' time on Earth and influenced his ministry. The occupation of Israel by Rome, the Maccabean revolt, the silence of the prophets, and the rise of the Pharisees in Judaism, to name a few. Jesus' life on Earth was constrained by time, his external environment, and many events preceding his time, yet through his surrender to the will of the Father, came to transcend all of it. But it was only through his surrender in the garden, where he said "not my will but yours be done,"[10] that his life came to be marked by the significance we now recognize it for.

If Jesus is our model for what a life of surrender is, then we can begin to see that a posture of surrender is the key to experiencing our life, and especially our careers, to the fullest. We begin to see that "when a person finds his high calling in life, it doesn't feel like he has taken control; it feels like he has surrendered control."[11] We recognize that "everybody has a 'fixed fate' set (perhaps) by his birth, and his purpose is not to find a new fate, but to adjust to it."[12] When we're surrendered to God, we begin to move with the current of God's sovereignty instead of fighting to get what *we* want. I think that why so many people feel stuck in their careers or have a

---

8. Buford, *Halftime*, 51.
9. John 3:30 (ESV)
10. Luke 22:42 (NIV)
11. Brooks, *Second Mountain*, 304.
12. Leithart, "Jane Austen, Public Theologian."

pervading sense of going against the grain is because they're trying to fight God's will and stay in control of our lives. We continue to see ourselves as the protagonist of whatever our calling might be, instead of God. We see ourselves more like an idealized version of David slaying all the armies that he encountered, instead of seeing the providence of God that led David through all the ups and downs from the shepherd's field to the throne of Israel.

Why so many of us continue trying to live with ourselves as the main character comes down to a mistaken view of what freedom is and what will lead to our greatest happiness. We're so used to control that we think freedom is the ability to do whatever we want and that any obstruction of that freedom is a source of unhappiness. Naturally, the call to surrender and live not on our own terms feels like the opposite of that, even though we get constant reminders in life that we're not in control, further impairing our sense of freedom and therefore our happiness. But what if a life of surrender to God would actually lead to the greatest amount of freedom that we could ever experience?

To see this, we turn back to Tolstoy, where he paints a contrast between the appearance of freedom and what he terms inevitability. The appearance of freedom is where our actions are the ones that appear to encounter the fewest obstacles, whereas inevitability is a function of the extent that we're connected to the world around us, the constraint of time on us, and our dependence on prior causes.[13] True freedom is thus where we are outside of time and outside of space and in the absence of cause. While none of these can be true for humans, they are true for God. And so, as we enter into a posture of surrender to God, we partner with the only truly free being in existence, outside of time and space, and allow our lives to be determined by a chain of events that flow out of his freedom. There is thus a harmony between the inevitability of our external environment, as authored by God, and our experience of freedom in communion with God. It's in this dynamic that our surrender to God allows him to lead us through a history of inevitability where we encounter the fewest obstacles—according

---

13. Tolstoy, *War and Peace*, 1299–1303.

to his design—and thus are able to experience the greatest sense of freedom. We encounter only the obstacles that God allows into our path, instead of the ones we place there ourselves. Or as Tolstoy puts it succinctly, "In the present case it is . . . necessary to renounce a freedom that does not exist, and to recognize a dependence of which we are not conscious."[14] But it is a dependence, a surrender, that brings life and freedom to us, instead of the opposite of what we think it will do. As Dallas Willard puts it, "The self-denial of Matthew 16:24 and elsewhere in the Gospels is always the surrender of a lesser, dying self for a greater eternal one—the person God intended in creating you."[15]

Biblically, we see this in the book of Psalms: "He makes me lie down in green pastures. He leads me beside still waters. He restores my soul. He leads me in paths of righteousness for his name's sake."[16] The psalm is describing the experiential encounter of surrender to God by the psalmist, as God leads him to experience the freedom that comes from being guided through the inevitability they find themselves in during the present. It's the experience of someone receiving freedom from the one who is free. We thus find in a life of surrender that "it really is good for you to surrender control and, in the process, come more fully to your senses—those senses that enable you to be aware of life's adventures and rewards."[17]

Arriving at a posture of surrender is synonymous with living a life of faith; you can't live a life of faith unless you're surrendered to the will of God. And a life of control is opposed to a life of faith. For so many people, we've reduced faith to something that we're in control of, where faith is just that period of waiting before we get what we want. We have faith that we'll get the promotion, our businesses will succeed, we'll catch a big break in our acting careers, or get the house we've dreamed of. But we haven't made space for a type of faith where our lives our filled with things we had never

---

14. Tolstoy, *War and Peace*, 1306.
15. Willard, *Renovation of the Heart*, 68.
16. Ps 23:1–3 (ESV)
17. Buford, *Halftime*, 37.

dreamt of. In fact, true faith does not know what's coming next. But when God is the author of the story, we don't need to know what comes next because "the only haven of safety [is] to have no other will, no other wisdom, than to follow the Lord wherever he leads."[18]

The chief reason that we refuse to surrender our lives is down to the mistaken belief that we know the best path and destination for our flourishing. We not only see ourselves as in control, but we also see ourselves as the person most well-positioned to figure out how to live our best lives, not the God of creation who knew us before conception. We pin our hopes and expectations on our dreams, our plans, our work, and our accomplishments, only to be consistently let down by them and desiring something more. "The idea that freedom consists in doing as one wills is a dead end. As finite beings, we don't possess the means to fulfill ourselves."[19] This reality reflects Jesus warning to us that "all who are obsessed with being secure in life will lose it all—including their lives. But those who let go of their lives and surrender them to me will discover true life."[20] It's this disconnect between our experience of a life of control and a hunger for something more that demonstrates that "there is an enormous gap between what we think we can do and what God calls us to do. Our ideas of what we can do or want to do are trivial; God's ideas for us are grand."[21]

Additionally, we fail to surrender our lives to God because we don't believe that he's as good as he says he is. We may not consciously say that we don't fully believe in God's goodness, but whenever we choose to live in accordance with our will and desires without consideration for God's will, we implicitly admit that we know better than God. Or rather, we make decisions that say that we don't believe that what God wants for our lives is better than what we want. Therefore, to surrender to God, we need to believe in God's goodness with our entire soul. Scripture is filled with

---

18. Willard, *Renovation of the Heart*, 143.
19. Adubato, "Metaphysical Promise of a Consumer Society."
20. Luke 17:33 (TPT)
21. Peterson, *Run with the Horses*, 49.

passages describing the perfect goodness of God: "The Lord, the Lord, the compassionate and gracious God, slow to anger, abounding in love and faithfulness,"[22] "Oh, give thanks to the Lord, for He is good! For His mercy endures forever,"[23] "The Lord is good to all; he has compassion on all he has made,"[24] "Every good gift and every perfect gift is from above, and comes down from the Father of lights, with whom there is no variation or shadow of turning,"[25] "He loves righteousness and justice; the earth is full of the goodness of the Lord,"[26] "Oh, taste and see that the Lord is good; blessed is the man who trusts in Him!"[27] "Teach me to do Your will, for You are my God; Your Spirit is good. Lead me in the land of uprightness."[28] It's only when we begin to believe that God truly is good that we can step into experiencing how great his desires for our lives really are. Thus, when the reality of God's goodness comes to fill our being, surrender then becomes a joyful response to God's will, rather than a grudging acceptance.

It's only when we begin embracing the life of surrender that we can begin to embrace the reality of God's grand ideas for our lives. We must, "in the end . . . accept, gratefully, [our] ordained roles, [our] 'fixed' fate."[29] As David Brooks writes, "It is a paradox that when people are finding themselves they often have a sensation that they are letting go and surrendering themselves."[30] Or as Bob Buford describes it, "At some moment I did answer Yes to Someone—or Something—and from that hour I was certain that existence is meaningful and that, therefore, my life, in self-surrender, had a goal."[31] Staying stuck in a life of control leads us to fall

22. Exod 34:6 (NIV)
23. 1 Chr 16:34 (NIV)
24. Ps 145:9 (NIV)
25. Jas 1:17 (NKJV)
26. Ps 33:5 (NASB)
27. Ps 34:8 (NKJV)
28. Ps 143:10 (NKJV)
29. Leithart, "Jane Austin, Public Theologian."
30. Brooks, *Second Mountain*, 70.
31. Buford, *Halftime*, 112.

short of God's ambition for our lives, whereas surrendering to God positions us to go further and faster than we can on our own and arrive at destinations we had never imagined before. Going farther and to unknown destinations doesn't mean we get more of what we already want, however. It doesn't mean you just supersize your pre-existing ambition. As Eugene Peterson writes, "Living by faith does not mean living with applause; living by faith does not mean playing on the winning team; living by faith demands readiness to live by what cannot be seen or controlled or predicted."[32] And it's in this life of living by what cannot be seen, controlled, or predicted that we encounter what we actually desire. What so many of us crave in our work lives is to experience the transcendent, but it's only at the intersection of our finite human efforts and infinite divine providence that this connection exists. But for our careers to have room for God to show up in them, we must let go of the sense of control that implicitly tells God that he isn't welcome.

Importantly, while a life of surrender allows God to work in such a way as to transcend our circumstances, it also means we can embrace our individual contexts and find meaning in them. While we are not truly free, nor are we the main characters of our story, Leo Tolstoy also makes the point that history, or the "movement of nations," is explained by the sum result of the activity of *everyone* participating in the events described, not by the power or intellectual activity of great people. Therefore, we all have a role to play in the movement of nations, as directed by God. We thus realize that strength is not how we imagined it, in terms of our influence over events or people but that "the strongest human will is always the one that is surrendered to God's will and acts with it."[33] Thus, as we surrender to God, we can accept the external world that we find ourselves in, the time we are subject to, and the events leading up to our current position but now see everything around us as the setting that God ordained for the story that he was writing about our life. We no longer have to fight the strokes of God's pen but willingly accept the calling he has in mind for us wherever we find

---

32. Peterson, *Run with the Horses*, 196.
33. Willard, *Renovation of the Heart*, 152.

ourselves in his story of humanity. It's "at this point you just let go of the wheel. You stop asking, What do I want? And start asking, what is life asking of me."[34] We see that "we are God's handiwork, created in Christ Jesus to do good works, which God prepared in advance for us to do."[35]

In surrender, we find the reconciliation between our individual circumstances and the sovereign will of God through the ages. As Jamie Winship puts it, "Above all else, though, Jesus will call you into the true identity he has given you before the foundation of the world."[36] And at the same time as we increasingly accept this reality, as we surrender our lives in exchange for the life that God has for us, we begin to sense God's hand at work, carrying our lives wherever he wants us to be. We begin to live as Paul described his own life to the Galatians: "I have been crucified with Christ. It is no longer I who live, but Christ who lives in me,"[37] and as a result, accept that "only one truth applies to all: the ultimate sacrifice we should make should be the whole of ourselves to God. And then we should simply let life take its course."[38] It is this way of living, where it is Christ living in us, that is the way that God designed our lives to be experienced, and particularly our careers.

But what does it look like to practically live a life of surrender? How can I better understand what it means for Christ to live in me? Let me explain through two examples.

In John Ortberg's *If You Want to Walk on Water You've Got to Get Out of the Boat*, he describes how birds have three methods of flight. The first method of flight is known as flapping, where birds are "keeping their wings in constant motion to counteract gravity." While "flapping keeps you up in the air [. . .] it is a lot of work." In this example, flapping is representative of the life of control. It may feel like we're expending a lot of energy or that we're in constant motion, but we are merely staying where we are.

34. Brooks, *Second Mountain*, 70.
35. Eph 2:10 (NIV)
36. Winship, *Living Fearless*, 114.
37. Gal 2:20 (ESV)
38. Sittser, *Water from a Deep Well*, 268.

Next, there is gliding, where if a "bird builds up enough speed, then coasts downward a while . . . Reality in the form of gravity sets in quickly. Gliding is nice, but it does not last." Gliding is about as good as our careers can get when we're living a life of control. We may experience a temporary burst of speed, either due to luck or some exceptionally hard work, but it's only ever a temporary phenomenon. The gravity of life will eventually overcome us at a certain point. Lastly, there is soaring, where capable birds can "[catch] rising currents of warm air . . . and without moving a feather soar up to great heights. They just soar on invisible columns of rising air."[39] This is the life of surrender. The kind of life where we soar up to great heights without moving a feather, a journey where God is the force that empowers our journey, not ourselves. Importantly, only certain types of birds are capable of soaring—they need to have wings strong enough to catch the currents. And so it is with us, we can't ride God's currents in our lives unless we're capable, unless we accept a life of surrender to him.

It is interesting to reflect on the image of Christ's body on the cross with the image of a soaring bird in mind. Like a bird with its wings outstretched as it flies along great currents of air, on the cross, we see Jesus arms spread out in a posture of total surrender to the Father. From a worldly perspective, this looks like death, but the reality is that Jesus is soaring on his faith in the Father. It's in the moment of weakness, in complete dependence and surrender to God that Jesus is the most alive and most completely fulfilling his calling on Earth.

In 2012, God also gave me a vision of what the life of surrender looks like while in a time of silent contemplation. The vision began with me standing on a flat sheet of ice that extended as far as the eye could see. There was nothing on the horizon that I could see. Suddenly, the ice beneath me began to crack, and I fell into the water. My first instinct was to grab on to the edge of the ice and pull myself out, but the more I fought, the harder it felt to stay out of the water. Finally, I relented and was completely submersed and began sinking into the depths of the water. I couldn't tell how deep

---

39. Ortberg, *If You Want to Walk on Water*, 185–86.

the water was, only that it was beyond my capacity to find out on my own. It was at this point that the Spirit told me that the water is God's love for us. The extent of it is beyond human comprehension. Despite this, we fight submitting to it with all of our insufficient ability. We fear that we are not in control of our destiny, but when the ice beneath us cracks, there is nothing available to save us if we feel that we are in control of our lives. However, as I was floating in the water, the more that I released control of my destiny, the more I sank into the unknown depths of the water. And the lower I went, the more I was at the mercy of currents that I could not control. As I sank, I thought to myself, how will I breathe underwater? But then at that moment, I took a breath of life that felt deeper and more fulfilling than I had ever known. And as I began to grow accustomed to letting go of control, and breathing in the life that was God's love, I sensed that I was now being carried by the currents through the depths of the sea.

There is a current of God's love through history that he is inviting us to swim in or soar on. The only question is, will you say yes to it? Will you "trust in the Lord with all your heart and lean not on your own understanding; in all your ways submit to him, and [believe] he will make your paths straight."[40] Will you trust that he has a life for you far beyond what you can build for yourself? This is the essence to life in the Spirit, whether we take God's promises at his word or whether we settle for our vain attempts at accomplishing what he promised to do for us. This is the heart of surrender. The only question then is, will you surrender?

AUTHOR'S REFLECTION

For as long as I can remember, I have been a goal-oriented person. Through some combination of temperament, my abilities, and God's work in my life, I've been able to focus my mind on a target and work through all of the ups and downs along the way to achieving what I set out for myself. Early in my career, this was

---

40. Prov 3:5–6 (NIV)

extremely helpful for my journey of becoming an independent adult. I finished university, got my first career job, and then was promoted. I completed a three-year professional examination program that was self-led and then was able to break into a new field of finance by teaching myself how to build financial models in Excel.

Part of all of these early achievements was good, but part of it was bad, especially from the perspective of life as a Christian. Unfortunately, what I instinctively came to believe was that if I put in the work and prayed about whatever goal I had in mind, it was bound to happen. Growing up in a late Western culture that emphasizes the importance of realizing one's own individual dreams and ambitions probably didn't help either. Essentially, I had confused my own dreams for my life with God's will for my life because he allowed a number of things into my life that I had asked for.

At a certain point, God stopped opening the doors that I prayed he would open. To put it mildly, this was an extremely disorienting period of my life, especially after experiencing so many answered prayers prior to that. But what it did reveal was the shallowness of my relationship with God. I had thought that as long as what I asked for wasn't obviously sinful, God would give me whatever I wanted. In other words, I had complete free reign over my life, providing that I avoided the obviously bad things I wasn't supposed to do as a Christian. It's only now that I can see how immature that mindset is, never mind all of the unconscious and un-biblical assumptions about my life and God that were behind those unfulfilled prayer requests.

In blunt terms, I still thought that I was in control of my life. Looking back, it's almost painful to notice that I never actually asked God what he thought of what I was asking for. Or even further, I never bothered to ask him what he wanted me to do. I was just doing whatever I wanted, sending up prayers, and waiting for the door to open or close based on what God thought about something I wanted for my life. What a slow process, when I could've just asked him!

What's sad about this way of living is what it unintentionally said about God. Without saying a word, my actions implied that I knew more than God about who I am and what the future held, and that I didn't believe he was actually as good as he said he is. I was relying on myself to figure all of that out instead of going straight to the source. Fortunately, God in his mercy closed the doors I had been trying to open for myself and led me to where I had actually wanted to be, which was surrendered to his will for my life.

I can assure you, however, that surrender doesn't come easily. I'm a recovering control freak after all. But what I can tell you is that surrender is far more life-giving than being in control. There is simply so much less that I have to worry about or take care of for myself now. Surrender feels like the easy yoke that Jesus talks about, and it's much easier to simply trust in God's good plans when things seem difficult than trying to fix everything yourself. I feel more like myself too. Or more accurately, I feel more like the person that God created me to be. The things I do feel like an outpouring of something set deep inside my soul, rather than fighting an uphill battle all by myself. There is peace that comes from knowing that wherever I find myself is a place that God has already gone before me to lead me to. And as I lean more into surrendering my life to Christ, I'm realizing more and more that what matters is obedience, and not the outcome.

DISCUSSION QUESTIONS

1. To what extent do you believe that you're in control of your life?
2. Do you believe that you're the main character of your career? Reflect on why you answered the way you did.
3. Why do you not believe that God has a greater plan for your life than your own?
4. What aspects of your life might God be trying to weave into his story?

9

Conclusion

As we've seen, becoming mature in our workplaces requires us to leave behind seven mindsets in favor of seven new ones. And with these seven transformations now in mind, we notice a few common themes.

First of these themes is that we all arrive at a default position of immaturity through a combination of the process of growing up where "what's important is that you start off by discovering the way God built you so that you can use your uniquely developed talents for him,"[1] messages that we receive from the world around us and a surface-level grasp of who God really is. And that wherever we find ourselves in the different aspects of immaturity, they each require stepping through a counterintuitive paradigm shift to experience work the way that our hearts desire to.

Second, there is an interwoven nature of the various postures of immaturity and maturity. We want certainty so we try and control our lives. We are striving to prove our capability to a watching world. We fail to be others-focused because we still evidence a scarcity mindset that doesn't believe our needs will be met no

---

1. Buford, *Halftime*, 104.

matter what. In contrast, we can embrace mystery when we're surrendered to God and his will for our lives. We readily accept self-transformation when we're content with who we are and what we receive in life. Other examples abound of this connectivity between the transformations.

Encouragingly, no matter where each of us finds ourselves, the general invitation to move forward in maturity or the specific invitations across the different aspects of maturity apply to us all. Every single one of us that works has an opportunity to experience their work differently when they say yes to God's invitations as they relate to our careers. Once we accept God's heart for our careers, our ambitions begin to change. Our goal is no longer the next step up the career ladder, a bigger business, or greater recognition. Our goal is now to simply take one small step towards mystery, contentment, vulnerability, abundance, others-focused living, self-transformation, and surrender. At the same time, we invite the Holy Spirit to lead us in this transformation of our work lives. We also accept the slow but worthwhile process of becoming increasingly like Christ at work, where we find the proper fusion between career (what we do), and character (who we are); this is the doing and being that humans were created for.

As we accept what it looks like to become mature Christians in our vocations, there are a few natural conclusions that can be reached.

You can receive a new heart to approach the work that you're already in. A heart that energizes your soul to do what you've always done but now from a completely different posture. Nothing around you has changed, but you have changed internally, and therefore everything about your work is different now. You now find the proper integration between what you've been called to do and who God designed you to be. David Brooks describes a transformed life this way: "Still others stay in their same jobs . . . but they are transformed. It's not about self anymore; it's about a summons. If they are principals, their joy is in seeing their teachers shine. If they work in a company, they no longer seem themselves as managers but as mentors; their energies are devoted to helping

Conclusion

others get better. They want their organizations to be thick places, where people find purpose, not thin places, where people come just to draw a salary."[2]

You might now be able to step into something you feel that you've been called to but haven't been able to say yes to because of the idols and lies of immaturity that have held you back. Perhaps you've always wanted to have a specific job but never could follow through with it because of fears that God wouldn't provide enough to meet your needs, or because of how you thought people might think of you, or as a result of worry that you weren't fully equipped to do it. Maybe you simply need to spend less time at work to open up to what God really wants to use you for. Ultimately, any prospective change needs to be motivated by "finding your 'one thing' and, in the process, finding what the Bible calls a state of joy, or blessedness."[3] I bid good adventure to any of you that find yourselves resonating with this.

You could also gain a new perspective for how to make sense of your work when it doesn't feel like any of it makes any sense or nothing is going right. Maybe the chaos or failure that you're experiencing is exactly where God wants you to be, because he's doing a deeper work in you and inviting you into something greater than you ever could've imagined. These periods are immensely trying, but with the right perspective of our work, we can find peace in the present.

Regardless of whether we stay where we are, change careers, or learn to embrace suffering, "the key to a successful second half is not a change of jobs; it is a change of heart, a change in the way you view the world and order your life."[4] Or as Henri Nouwen writes, "Jesus does not speak about a change of activities, a change in contacts, or even a change of pace. He speaks about a change of heart. This change of heart makes everything different, even while everything appears to remain the same."[5]

2. Brooks, *Second Mountain*, xiv.
3. Buford, *Halftime*, 80.
4. Buford, *Halftime*, 97–98.
5. Nouwen, *Spiritual Life*, 14.

Wherever we find ourselves, and for all the future paths we may now dream for ourselves, I want to end our time together by homing in on the truth that is the foundation of this entire book. This truth strings all of the seven transformations together and is fundamental to our growth into mature workers. This truth is as follows: to experience work the way that God intended means we must start with an identity rooted in our position as sons and daughters of God. All of our joy from work flows out of our acceptance of this reality. Dissatisfaction at work follows our incomplete grasp of this truth. If we don't see our work through this lens, we risk trying to make ourselves look like God through our own efforts, instead of receiving the reality that we are already like him because of who he created us to be. We will try and build our own kingdoms instead of his. And we will suffer in the present as a result.

Further, holding our identities secure in our position as children of God is the basis upon which we receive our individual callings. As Jamie Winship writes, "We do not find our true self by seeking it, rather, we find it by seeking God."[6] We tend to get this part of our work lives backwards; we think our career is our calling, or how we find significance. But in fact, we find that our calling starts with God's declaration of our position as beloved sons and daughters of God in whom he is well-pleased. This is before we do anything that we're called to. We see this first and foremost in the life of Jesus. God declares his sonship before Jesus completes any of the works that he was called to do. But importantly, when Jesus was called, he already had a career. Similarly for us, we need to start with a right view of God and ourselves to receive our unique identity and calling, as "God will only call you a name he would call himself... He'll call you something that moves you forward in freedom. It's something that excites you, brings you joy and peace. Sometimes what God says about us is almost too beautiful to believe... The frequency resonates with your heart."[7]

---

6. Winship, *Living Fearless*, 105.
7. Winship, *Living Fearless*, 127.

Conclusion

When we look at our careers and how they relate to our callings in the life of Jesus, we can then see that Jesus' career was a stepping stone that brought him to his calling. We see this career and calling parallel dynamic throughout the Bible as well. To name a few examples:

Character	Career	Calling
Abraham	Shepherd	Father of Israel
Joseph	Administrator	Rescued Israel from famine
David	Warrior	King of Israel
Solomon	King	Built the Temple of God
Jesus	Carpenter	Messiah
Peter	Fisherman	Rock the Church was built on
Paul	Tentmaker	Spread the Gospel to gentiles

The career/calling parallelism is not an either/or construct, however. We don't quit our careers so that we can live our callings. It's a both/and reality; our careers and callings work together. But, if we settle for only a career, marked by the postures of immaturity, we will miss out on our callings. In Peter Leithart's essay on Jane Austen's *Mansfield Park*, he contrasts career and calling in terms of acting and vocation, where "'vocation' is set in direct contrast to 'acting.' Both have to do with taking on or playing 'roles,' but the meaning of 'role' in the two cases is quite different. An actor might adopt many different roles, none of which defines who he is." Actors have no "'fixed fate' in life," whereas someone with a calling is "in a more profound sense [someone who] has been chosen . . . For a called man or woman, his or her role is not a mask that can be removed at will. The mask sticks so closely to his face as to be permanent."[8] We too have a choice between the fixed fate of a calling and the fleeting nature of a career. Settling for a career therefore causes us to lose sight of the singular reason that God created us and subjects us to fleeting senses of purpose and mission rather than recognizing a reason for being that transcends the temporary nature of earthly life. To live only for career would

8. Leithart, "Jane Austen, Public Theologian."

be like an alternate version of Jesus that stayed as a carpenter his entire life, believing that the buildings he was constructing were all that God was calling him to. Our invitation is to choose careers aligned with our callings, where our identity informs what we do. As Jamie Winship writes, "I know what vocations enable and empower [my] identity."[9]

This transformation of career into calling that occurs alongside the journey from immaturity to maturity starts with understanding who God is, and who he says that we are as his children. That reality is the fuel that powers us into the maturity that produces something beyond ourselves with eternal impact in partnership with God. It's this identity that makes us open to mystery, content, accept our vulnerability, believe in God's abundance, serve as others-focused people, pursue self-transformation, and surrender to God's will, all of which are needed to fulfill our callings.

But while our careers and callings are interrelated, they are different in important ways. When we step into our callings, we will experience much fruit in our lives, especially in terms of how we qualitatively experience our life at work. However, the fruit that we produce out of our callings will differ from that of our careers. With our careers, we get used to short-term, measurable results. We can see, taste, touch, smell, and hear the work of our hands on a regular basis. Our callings are not like that. If anything, the best image that we get of callings is a "foretaste of future glory,"[10] as Paul describes it. Our experience of our callings will simply be an inkling of what's to come on this side of heaven. What this means is that we will not see the full extent of what God does with our calling while we're on Earth. We must go beyond "the rational, which takes in what can be seen and measured" and embrace "the sphere beyond the rational, which defied human comprehension and belongs in the realm of the gods."[11] We are to commit to callings that "point to an ideal that is far in the distance and can't be

---

9. Winship, *Living Fearless*, 29.
10. Rom 8:23 (NLT)
11. Buford, *Halftime*, 57.

CONCLUSION

achieved in a life"[12] where we, in the words of Henry Moore, "have a task, something you devote your entire life to, something you bring everything to, every minute of every day for the rest of your life" and where "the most important thing is, it must be something you cannot possibly do."[13] Our work that we give ourselves over to "unfolds over a long period of time" where "each decision, event, experience, and sacrifice, which might have seemed small and insignificant at the time, prepared them for the next."[14] "But constancy, perseverance, a long obedience in one direction—this, of course, is precisely the difference between acting a role [career] and accepting a role as a vocation [calling]."[15] Because ultimately, our callings are not about us but about God, and therefore we are playing our role in a part of a story that extends into eternity. Therefore, "if we diligently perform the work that God has called us to, we can suffer delay, and even death, without fear. The work will endure, because it is His work."[16]

Abraham didn't see the nation of Israel that he was the father of, Moses died in the wilderness, Paul didn't see the full growth of the church to gentile nations, Jesus left earth before the kingdom he was sent to usher in became manifest with the establishment and growth of the church, and Mary Slessor worked for over a decade as a missionary before she saw her first convert to Christianity.[17] Because of the context we live in, we all seem to want to be around to see the fruit of whatever we do, but we have to accept that our role in fulfilling our callings will not always be connected to the outcome of it, and that's the way God intended it, because "Christians are commanded to live in a way that doesn't make sense unless God exists."[18]

---

12. Brooks, *Second Mountain*, 295.
13. Brooks, *Second Mountain*, 295.
14. Sittser, *Water from a Deep Well*, 278.
15. Leithart, "Jane Austen, Public Theologian."
16. Beck, "Anti-Fragile Brendan Eich."
17. Sittser, *Water from a Deep Well*, 271.
18. Brooks, *Second Mountain*, 223.

So as we stand on the precipice of walking into our callings, we are like the Israelites at the edge of the promised land with the Jordan River at our feet. We have all of God's promises in mind about the promised land, but the way forward looks like sheer folly. A land full of certain danger feels like going backwards compared to the desert and Egypt. But life at its fullest, experiencing the career satisfaction that we're looking for, means we need to go through the river. It means going through the river, and like Jesus, receiving a secure identity that will lead us wherever we need to go, provide for all of our needs along the way, and produce fruit that will last for eternity. The only question left is this: will you take the next step?

Bibliography

Adubato, Stephen. "The Metaphysical Promise of the Consumer Society." First Things, Sep. 3, 2024. https://www.firstthings.com/web-exclusives/2024/09/the-metaphysical-promise-of-the-consumer-society.

Barth, Karl. *Church Dogmatics*. Vol. 3 in *The Doctine of Reconciliation: Part One*. Edinburgh: T. & T. Clark, 1956.

Beck, Andrew. "The Anti-Fragile Brendan Eich." First Things, April 12, 2024. https://www.firstthings.com/web-exclusives/2024/04/the-anti-fragile-brendan-eich.

Brooks, David. *The Second Mountain: The Quest for a Moral Life*. New York: Penguin Random House, 2020.

Buford, Bob. *Halftime: Moving from Success to Significance*. Grand Rapids: Zondervan, 2015.

Comer, John Mark. "Active & Passive Spirituality." Sermon, Bridgetown Church, Portland, OR. May 19, 2019.

———. *Garden City: Work, Rest, and the Art of Being Human*. Grand Rapids: Zondervan, 2015.

———. *Practicing the Way: Be with Jesus. Become Like Him. Do as He Did*. Colorado Springs: WaterBrook, 2024.

———. *The Ruthless Elimination of Hurry*. Colorado Springs: WaterBrook, 2019.

Duarte, Nancy. *Data Story: Explain Data and Inspire Action Through Story*. Ideapress, 2019.

Elkins, Kathleen. "Warren Buffett Simplifies Investing with a Baseball Analogy." Feb. 2, 2017. https://www.cnbc.com/2017/02/02/warren-buffett-simplifies-investing-with-a-baseball-analogy.html.

Friedman, Edwin H. *A Failure of Nerve: Leadership in the Age of the Quick Fix*. New York: Church, 2017.

Gladwell, Malcolm. *Outliers: The Story of Success*. New York: Little, Brown and Company, 2008.

BIBLIOGRAPHY

Greenleaf Center for Servant Leadership. "What Is Servant Leadership?" https://www.greenleaf.org/what-is-servant-leadership/.

Harrison, Nathan. "Sabbath as Resistance." Westside Church, Vancouver, BC. Oct. 30, 2022.

Hoffer, Eric. *Reflections on the Human Condition*. Titusville, NJ: Hopewell, 2006.

Jethani, Skye. *With: Reimagining the Way You Relate to God*. Nashville: Thomas Nelson, 2011.

Kelly, Thomas Raymond. *A Testament of Devotion*. San Francisco: HarperSanFrancisco, 1992.

Kennedy, Dana. "The Fame He Craved Came, but It Wasn't Enough." *New York Times*, Aug. 18, 2002. https://www.nytimes.com/2002/08/18/arts/film-the-fame-he-craved-came-but-it-wasn-t-enough.html.

Lawrence, Brother. *The Practice of the Presence of God: Being Conversations and Letters of Nicholas Herman of Lorraine*. Eastford, CT: Martino Fine Books, 2016.

Leithart, Peter. "Jane Austen, Public Theologian." First Things, Jan. 2004. https://www.firstthings.com/article/2004/01/jane-austen-public-theologian.

Manning, Brennan. *Abba's Child: The Cry of the Heart for Intimate Belonging*. Colorado Springs: NavPress, 2015.

Maxwell, John. *How Successful People Grow: 15 Ways to Get Ahead in Life*. New York: Center Street, 2014.

Merton, Thomas. *New Seeds of Contemplation*. New York: New Directions, 1961.

———. *The Wisdom of the Desert*. New York: New Directions, 1960.

Mulholland, M. Robert. *Invitation to a Journey: A Road Map for Spiritual Formation*. Downers Grove, IL: InterVarsity, 2016.

Nouwen, Henri. *The Spiritual Life: Eight Essential Titles*. New York: HarperCollins, 2016.

Ortberg, John. *If You Want to Walk on Water You've Got to Get Out of the Boat*. Grand Rapids: Zondervan, 2001.

Owens, Craig. "Susanna Wesley On Prayer." Oct. 30, 2014. https://craigtowens.com/2014/10/30/susanna-wesley-on-prayer/.

Palmer, Parker. *Let Your Life Speak*. San Francisco: Jossey-Bass, 2000.

Peterson, Eugene. *Run with the Horses: The Quest for Life at Its Best*. Downers Grove: InterVarsity, 2019.

Rolheiser, Ronald. *Sacred Fire: A Vision for a Deeper Human and Christian Maturity*. New York: Image, 2014.

Rosenman, Ray H., and Meyer Friedman. *Type A Behavior and Your Heart*. New York: Knopf, 1974.

Scazzero, Peter. *Emotionally Healthy Spirituality: It's Impossible to Be Spiritually Mature While Remaining Emotionally Immature*. Grand Rapids: Zondervan, 2017.

Sittser, Gerald. *Water from a Deep Well: Christian Spirituality from Early Martyrs to Moder Missionaires*. Downers Grove: InterVarsity, 2007.

Bibliography

Solzhenitsyn, Aleksandr. *The Gulag Archipelago: 1918–56*. London: Harvill, 2003.

Spurgeon, C. H. *Spurgeon's Lectures to His Students*. Edited by David Otis Fuller. Grand Rapids: Zondervan, 1945.

Staton, Tyler. *Praying Like Monks, Living Like Fools: An Invitation to the Wonder and Mystery of Prayer*. Grand Rapids: Zondervan, 2022.

Tolstoy, Leo. *War and Peace*. New York: Oxford University Press, 1998.

Wikipedia. "Servant Leadership." https://en.wikipedia.org/wiki/Servant_leadership.

Willard, Dallas. *Renovation of the Heart: Putting on the Character of Christ*. Colorado Springs: NavPress, 2012.

Winship, Jamie. *Living Fearless: Exchanging the Lies of the World for the Liberating Truth of God*. Grand Rapids: Revell, 2022.

www.ingramcontent.com/pod-product-compliance
Lightning Source LLC
Chambersburg PA
CBHW071214160426
43196CB00012B/2301

"This book takes the reader on a journey toward spiritual maturity that involves a paradigm shift in outlook or social imaginary. Jeff Mayhew highlights the strategic nature of the workplace as a theatre of spiritual formation. It offers a roadmap toward depth of character."

—**GORDON E. CARKNER**, graduate and faculty ministry coordinator, Outreach Canada

"Struggling to connect your career to your faith? Read this book! Jeff Mayhew offers a master class in discipleship for the working person. As Jeff demonstrates, the workplace is formative in our journey to Christlikeness. He deftly illustrates why and how to shift the default assumptions of success and control to a life of faith, surrender, and alignment with God's Kingdom."

—**TIMOTHY ERNST**, marketplace mentor, The Navigators of Canada

"Many people today feel disenchanted with simply climbing the corporate ladder and find themselves longing for something deeper. Jeff offers a clear and compelling alternative, rooted in the person and way of Jesus. His passion for helping others discover God's presence in their work shines through every chapter as he guides readers toward a path of joy, fulfillment, and more of what we truly need."

—**NATHAN HARRISON**, pastor

"In *When Forward Feels Backward*, Jeff invites us to see the workplace as a significant arena for spiritual formation and transformation. Reflecting on his own journey, he takes readers on an exploratory adventure, challenging us to think deeply and embrace a Spirit-led posture amid the twists and turns of work and our unfolding careers. Offering an alternative narrative, this book equips us to navigate and wayfind through this vital part of our lives, inspiring alignment with God's purpose and discovering the invitation to true freedom in the workplace."

—**Stephen Mulder**, co-founder, Missional Labs